WISDOM AND MINISTRY

The Call to Leadership

Michael Sadgrove

First published in Great Britain in 2008

Society for Promoting Christian Knowledge
36 Causton Street
London SW1P 4ST

British Library Cataloguing-in-Publication Data
A catalogue record for this book is available from the British Library

ISBN 978–0–281–05997–3

1 3 5 7 9 10 8 6 4 2

Typeset by Kenneth Burnley, Wirral, Cheshire
Printed in Great Britain by Ashford Colour Press

Produced on paper from sustainable forests

For Tony with love

Contents

Contents

Preface

This book had its beginnings in retreat addresses given to deacon and priest candidates in the Diocese of Durham in 2005. I am grateful to Tom Wright, the Bishop of Durham, for this privilege. The material has been considerably rewritten and elaborated; five chapters are completely new. As an epilogue, I have included the sermon I preached at the ordination of deacons that year which tries to encapsulate the wisdom theme of the retreat.

Inevitably, much of what I have learned from my own experience surfaces in this book. I want to acknowledge the debt I owe to the many people who have accompanied me on this journey: clergy who have been inspiring role models, colleagues in the places where I have been (and am) a priest, and a long line of spiritual advisers and mentors. I am especially thinking, with deep gratitude, of my wife and children who see the truth of ordained ministry from the inside.

The Reverend Tony Bryer generously laid aside his own writing projects in the closing days of his sabbatical leave to read the text and comment on it. I am grateful for this and for so much else. This book is dedicated to him as a wise minister and the best of friends.

Michael Sadgrove, The Deanery, Durham
Advent 2007

Introduction: wisdom and ministry in the twenty-first century

—————➤•◦•◄—————

I remember vividly that on the day of my own ordination I was called 'Sir' for the first time by a man old enough to be my father. That experience was elaborated by a senior Churchwarden who remarked, when conducting me round the parish as a prospective incumbent, 'We place Vicars here on a pedestal.' I felt uncomfortable with that assertion and replied, 'I shall jump off.' 'You cannot jump off other people's pedestals, but you can look to your own and then ours will take care of themselves.'

(Michael Bowering, ed., *Priesthood Here and Now*, Newcastle Diocese, 1994, p. 95)

I became the incumbent of a traditional country market town in north-east England 25 years ago, though no one called me 'Sir'. However, I did find it strange and a little odd to be called 'Vicar'. 'Call me by my Christian name,' I said with a gaucheness that now makes me blush. Some did, but many did not. I mistook it for an inappropriate and outdated deference. While you might defer to a bishop or a duke (or both, in rural Northumberland), the relationship between people and priest seemed to me to call for something more relaxed and egalitarian. Pedestals were definitely out.

I now see that the matter is more complex and elusive. I was not as clear then as I later became about the difference between 'role' and 'person': the fundamental distinction between *what* we are and *who* we are. I also confused 'deference' with 'respect'. To find myself, as R. S. Thomas puts it in one of his poems, 'a vicar of large things in a small parish', was daunting enough, and I was not prepared for what it entailed (though in your early thirties, you don't imagine there is much you cannot do). To look to my own pedestal so that other people's would take care of themselves, as Bowering puts it, was something I only began to learn fitfully, often the hard way. It took time to be able to give an account, at least to myself, of what ordained ministry really *meant* and what respect was due to it.

It takes a lifetime to understand what a vocation means, just as it takes a lifetime to understand what marriage means (another lifelong vocation and just as much of a privileged mystery). Both must be inhabited from within: as Kierkegaard said of human life, it has to be lived forwards and understood backwards. The ordinal and the service of institution or licensing to a parish both make important, indeed vital, statements about the *tasks* of ministry. But they do not (and cannot) do more than hint at its deepest *meaning*, and how this is experienced both by the individual who has accepted the vocation to be a priest, and by the people he or she is called to serve. This is what the awkward language of the 'pedestal' seems to point to. It stands for the difficult task of finding a way of speaking with respect about the ordained ministry, and recognizing the inward consequences for 'vicars' themselves of being the subject of this kind of language and the projections that go with it.

What the ordained ministry is in itself, what ministers believe about their own role, and how they are perceived by others both within and beyond the Church, are, I believe, key questions today. Social science, in describing the behaviour of the clergy, finds clues there about the nature of organized religion and its function in society. Biographical studies that focus on the careers of the Church's leaders and shapers down the centuries, or on the hidden lives of the 'ordinary' clergy in their day-to-day ministry (which is often more interesting), shed light on how the Church has understood its mission in history. Examining how the nature and function of the ordained ministry is to be understood theologically has been a vital task addressed by all the churches, not least in the search for Christian unity.

While theology, history and social science are all important, however, this book is not a rigorous study of the nature of ordained ministry. Rather, it is an attempt to reflect on the *meaning* of ordained ministry as it is understood and experienced both by the Church and by the ordained themselves. Inevitably, the path my own ministry has taken is a large part of what I bring to this: meanings are personal as well as collective. It would be dishonest not to acknowledge how many themes in my own ministry have come together in this book. So it may be helpful to say something about my *curriculum vitae* at this point.

My first full-time job as a recently ordained priest in the mid-1970s was to teach the Old Testament at a theological college. I believed then, and still believe, that for the Church, the Hebrew Bible is not simply worth studying for itself, or as background to the New Testament, but offers a unique perspective on a religious community wrestling with issues of faith in a huge variety of human situations. Insofar as this book suggests connections between the Old Testament and the practice of ministry today, it is as I have revisited the wonderfully enriching experience of training ordinands 30 years ago. Ever since then, how ordinands are prepared for ministry, or 'formed' as we now say, has occupied much of my time and energy. The world and the Church have changed hugely in 30 years, but not the vital search, as I see the task of formation, for ways to marry biblical and theological literacy with maturity in the emotional and spiritual life.

After some years I moved to the other end of the country to a first incumbency. It was salutary to become a parish priest and learn for myself something of the nature of the ministry for which I had helped prepare others. In a country market town, the parish priest is still (or was in the 1980s) something of a 'parson', with a role towards an entire human community, not simply those who attend church. A first living is always a place of truth: for me, at least, it was where I learned more about ministry and about myself than at any time before or since. I think this is because it is where the vision with which ministry begins is tested, sometimes brutally, against the hard facts of responsibility. (To go back to the analogy of marriage, it is perhaps comparable to the arrival of children.) In an incumbency, there is nowhere to hide our inadequacies or find shelter at times of stress or distress.

Later on, I became a residentiary canon at a cathedral, with the task, as precentor, of devising and organizing liturgy for ordinations. These occasions are always a high point in the life of a cathedral and diocese as well as the candidates and their families and parishes. It required me to think carefully about what an ordination service is *for*, and how it has a 'formative' function not simply for the candidates but for everyone. It necessitated looking at what messages about ministry an ordination should (and shouldn't) convey. All this raised key questions about how ordination candidates are helped to negotiate the rite-of-passage from 'laity' to 'clergy', something to which the Church does not always pay as much attention as it should.

Having been a dean now for well over a decade, in two cathedrals, I have had to think about priesthood in a larger, more public way. A cathedral is a place where the exercise of ministry is particularly open to scrutiny, both by the Church whose 'big space' it is, and by wider society for whom it is often a portal for religion and where what is on offer is taken to stand for Christianity as a whole. Cathedrals provide many dangerous opportunities for pedestals, to go back to my opening remarks: so the need to 'look to our own' is crucial. The strengths and shortcomings of cathedral clergy are very visible: how they preside at liturgy, how they preach, how they care for people (perhaps even *whether* they do), how they represent Christianity in public, and not least, how well they relate to their ordained and lay colleagues as a team. Moreover, a cathedral is a sign of 'public faith' where the gospel is spoken into the life of society: governance, the academy, the market-place and social need. This is not different in principle from the ministry of an incumbent, but it is more public. In a cathedral, there can be no collusion (as there can be in a parish) with the idea that a priest is merely a chaplain to a gathered congregation.

For most of my ministry, I have acted as a spiritual director to ordinands and clergy. Those I have tried to support and help have, wittingly or unwittingly, offered many perspectives on ministry I would not otherwise have had. They have helped me to fill out the picture my own experience has given me of what it is like to be ordained today as they have shared their joys, their pressures, their perplexities and their pain. I have tried to distil some of this in the ordination retreats I have led in different dioceses from time to time, those uniquely precious opportunities for reflection, prayer and common life charged with the heightened spiritual awareness that accompanies journeys across liminal places of transition.

In all this, I have become more and more aware of the need for wisdom, both for myself as a minister and for the Church as it wrestles with its challenges and tasks in our time. What clergy are and do is of course only a small part of what it means to be the Church: the invitation to become wise is addressed to all the baptized, indeed, all humanity. However, for better or worse, the leadership of any organization sets its tone, articulates its vision, inculcates its values. There are already a number of excellent books on how wisdom can inform and inspire discipleship, and some on wisdom in relation to education. *[common?]*

In this book I want specifically to explore how the wisdom literature of the Old Testament offers insights into our understanding of ordained ministry today. 'Wisdom' plays a key role in the Hebrew Bible, not least in the books traditionally regarded as wisdom literature such as Job, Proverbs, Ecclesiastes, the Song of Solomon and some of the psalms. However, its influence is far wider than those books of 'taught' wisdom alone. Some of the most powerful stories in the Old Testament seem to be told from a similar perspective, and illustrate the lessons of wisdom and folly through the careers of men like Joseph, David, Solomon and Daniel. Indeed, perhaps the entire Hebrew Bible, as a definitive collection or 'canon' of books, is the result of the 'wise' identifying those writings recognized as authoritatively 'wise' for the life of the Jewish community.

Yet in the Church's use of the Old Testament, wisdom literature is something of a poor relation compared to the law, the prophets and the psalms. It does not feature very much in the biblical readings at the Sunday service. We don't hear many sermons on wisdom. This is strange, given the importance wisdom has in the New Testament. St Paul says that the proclamation of the gospel is not 'a wisdom of this age' but is 'God's wisdom, secret and hidden, which God decreed before the ages' (1 Corinthians 2.6–7). The Corinthian letters spell out what it means to say that Christ is both 'the power of God and the wisdom of God' (1 Corinthians 1.24). This rich language draws directly on passages in the Hebrew Bible that speak of wisdom as God's handmaid in the creation of the world (Proverbs 8.22ff.) and therefore the origin of all human life, activity and intelligence. And just as the New Testament speaks of discipleship as walking in the path of the wisdom that is Christ himself, so in the Hebrew Bible to be wise means to be in a right relationship with the God who is both the source of all human wisdom and is wisdom himself. 'The fear of the Lord, that is wisdom,' says the book of Job (28.28). So wisdom speaks about the whole of life as given new meaning and direction by this divine gift. As Christians read these texts, they see foreshadowed the coming of God's wisdom into the world in the person of Christ, and his continuing presence in the Church as the Spirit of Truth.

If Christianity means becoming wise in Christ, then one way of looking at Christian ministry is to see it as the task of helping others to find this path of wisdom for themselves. Perhaps we could see in the wise of ancient Israel an apt model for the ordained ministry today. If 'wisdom' means among other things qualities like insight, perceptiveness, spiritual intelligence, theological discernment, if, indeed, it means ultimately becoming like God himself, we should (to take up the metaphor of Job 28) be quarrying this rich tradition of biblical literature to inform our understanding of ministry in the Church today. And this applies as much to *formation* for ministry, and to the way we devise ceremonies of ordination and transition into new ministries, as it does to its day-to-day practice.

In a speech at General Synod during the debate on the new Church of England ordination rites, I made a point about this. It came out of my concern that Old Testament readings at ordination services tend to be drawn from the 'call' narratives of prophets. Isaiah's temple vision (Isaiah 6.1–8) is the *locus classicus* of the prophet's call. His grand vision of the Lord 'high and lifted up', his humbling of himself in the light of his and his people's sin, the divine voice that asks, 'Whom shall I send, and who will go for us?', and his willing response, 'Here am I; send me!': these all seem tailor-made for an ordination or commissioning service. (At this point, I need to protest at how the integrity of this text is wrecked by ending the reading at that point, as is usually done. The passage concludes not with the prophet's words but with God's announcement of the message Isaiah is charged to deliver. This stark and terrible warning of judgement is, I suspect, very much *not* what is in the minds of most bishops and ordinands at that moment.)

However, the main point is this. It seems to me that to liken Anglican parochial ministry to the vocation of the prophets sets up a whole range of misleading and even damaging expectations. It assumes that visionary experience is somehow the norm, whereas it has probably always been highly exceptional, even in ancient Israel. It assumes that vocation springs from a divine encounter in which the voice of God is directly heard and responded to, whereas most people's experience is that it is a subtle process of formation and maturing, the 'discernment' of which by the Church takes a long time. It assumes (if the passage is read in full) that the 'normal' mode of ministry will be that of the prophetic oracle of judgement (to begin with) and promise; and while 'being prophetic' is a proper part of ordained ministry, clergy do not (and cannot) operate in this mode for most of the time.

I said in my speech to the Synod that I doubted that ordained ministry in the twenty-first century was remotely like the call to be an eighth-century Hebrew prophet. I thought it was therefore important at ordination services to broaden the range of Old Testament texts so as to suggest other metaphors (because this is what they are) of what it might mean to be a priest or a deacon in the Church of England. And while I don't deny that ministry has its prophetic dimension, nor that we each have to utter our own

'Yes' to God when he summons us, it seems to me that the wise in Israel are far closer to what we look for in the public ministers of our churches. Furthermore, we should align this suggestion with what is happening during the ordination prayer itself, when the bishop calls on God to 'send down the Holy Spirit upon your servant for the office and work of a deacon (or priest) in your Church'. This is nothing less than the invocation of *Hagia Sophia*, the holy, everlasting, life-giving Wisdom of God by which the world was made. The prayer is for this same creative, energizing power to surround, enlighten and equip ministers for their task.

What follows from this proposal that we should link ordained ministry with biblical wisdom? Four related themes emerge in this book.

First, the inward formation of the minister. Being wise as the prerequisite for helping others to become wise is utterly basic to Hebrew wisdom, both in the 'taught' books of wisdom and in its narrative, biographical forms. So I have a lot to say about the spiritual, emotional, intellectual and personal 'formation' of ministers, what they *are* as well as what they *do*. If, as Socrates says, 'the unreflected life is not worth living', then the ordained are *par excellence* those who should be living it and demonstrating its value. We all know that this does not simply happen, and is not miraculously imparted with the laying on of hands. It is hard won, the outcome of serious 'heart work'. Learning this *habitus* of wisdom seems to me to be an absolute priority for all ministers who are serious about their calling.

Second, ministry as a public activity. Hebrew wisdom appears to have evolved in court circles where the young were prepared for public office. The role of the wise in mentoring, advising and warning kings and rulers is not entirely clear, but there can be little doubt that it had a vital public function in Israel. In particular, the narratives of Joseph, David, Solomon and

Daniel all ask questions about what it means to be a wise and therefore effective leader, in many ways not far removed from the questions that leadership theory asks today. I have tried to make some connections into the world of ordained ministry, but wisdom insights can easily be transferred to leadership roles in other organizations as well. What I want to emphasize is that leadership in the Church is a *public role*. Clergy hold 'office', which is to say that they are authorized representatives of the Church not only as a faith community but also as an organization. I see this as a creative possibility before it is a burden (though it can be that), and try to explain why.

Third, the relationship between the public and personal worlds of the minister. In the narratives especially, the interplay of public and private is crucial. The stories of David and Solomon show how a distorted understanding of the self-in-role, especially the abuse of the privilege and power that any role confers, gets to be played out in public, sometimes disastrously. Wisdom, in the Hebrew Bible, means knowing oneself as a public figure in a role, and as a human person; therefore knowing oneself means understanding and living out with integrity the often difficult relationship between the two. Here, the pastoral care of the clergy, linked to wise support and mentoring, are indispensable not only for their own mental and spiritual health, but for the wellbeing of the whole Church.

Fourth, and drawing on the first three insights, I develop towards the end of the book the idea that *ordained ministry is to do with bearing public 'witness'*. It is obvious that like every Christian, a minister is ordained to bear witness to the gospel: this is his or her fundamental task. I want, however, to apply this to the myriad encounters a minister has with human life in all its complex variety, and suggest that he or she is specifically a 'witness' – on behalf of God, the Church and humanity – to pain, to the search for meaning, and to the gift of joy.

To do this convincingly, and with integrity, calls for real wisdom.

The book has two parts. In Part One, 'The tides of wisdom', I offer some character studies drawn from stories in the Old Testament that are told from a wisdom perspective: Solomon (as both a wise and a foolish leader), Joseph, Daniel and David. I believe that these stories offer distinctive insights for church leaders, because they are variously about leadership in confusing, complex or alien settings. I am not of course implying that ancient Egypt or Israel or Babylon where these stories are set are remotely like modern societies. But there are suggestive parallels that may speak to religious leaders in our own era facing what is often confusing, complex or alien in our own culture. In Part Two, 'Learning from wisdom', I explore insights drawn from the 'taught' wisdom books: Proverbs, Psalms 1 and 73, Job, Ecclesiastes and the Song of Solomon. These face squarely many of the issues which daily confront all human beings of every age, and which are therefore always going to be central to Christian ministry.

Probably, most readers of this book will be clergy and those offering for ordained ministry, though I should like to think that its themes are important for anyone in a leadership role in the Church. While I am writing as an Anglican priest (and I use the language of 'ordained minister', 'clergy' and 'priest' interchangeably), I have in mind the ordained ministers of any Christian Church. I also hope that anyone who is (understandably) puzzled or intrigued by why men and women should offer themselves for ordination in the twenty-first century will find food for thought here too.

Ultimately, the questions surrounding ordained ministry are questions for the whole Church, not simply the ordained and those close to them or with a responsibility for them. The Church gets the ministry it asks for (and deserves). Not to ask the right questions in discussions about the nature and resourcing of ordained ministry would be (and at times has been) a key theological and missiological failure.

One of France's greatest preachers, the seventeenth-century Bishop Bossuet, reflected on the nature of preaching. In one of his sermons, he spoke with his customary dazzling oratory about the preacher's awesome responsibility towards his people. Then with a rhetorical flourish he turned to his hearers and asked how they saw *their* responsibility. He said: 'Perhaps you are here to sit in judgement on my sermon – but at the Last Judgement you will have to answer for your part in it.' It is a profound theological and pastoral insight to realize that the sermon is an event shaped in both the pulpit and the pew. This is true not simply of preaching but of every aspect of public ministry. The Church in its entirety is wholly implicated in what the ordained do and are, whether for good or ill; for in them, its own priesthood as the body of Christ is focused and given visible expression.

Kierkegaard famously said that it is not the preacher who is the 'performer', but the hearer. The preacher is simply the prompter in the drama of human life as it is lived and performed before God. Ministry exists to 'prompt' that drama and coax human minds and hearts into life by pointing them to the hints, echoes and foresights of the kingdom of God, asking in effect, 'Do you see what I see?' It exists to lead and serve the Church's witness to the possibilities of justice, love and truth that the promise of the kingdom offers. Wisdom looks for what God intends for the good of his whole creation. This, and only this, is the beginning and end of ministry. Nothing else matters.

Part One

THE TIDES OF WISDOM

1

Knowing what to ask for:
Solomon (Part 1)

In Durham Cathedral there is a striking painting, recently commissioned for the building, by the contemporary artist Paula Rego. It shows Saint Margaret of Scotland, one of the most distinguished monarchs of the Middle Ages. Her connection with Durham Cathedral is that its first prior, Turgot, was her confessor and later wrote a biography of her. In the late summer of 1093, her husband Malcolm Canmore, King Malcolm III of Scotland, was in Durham to lay a foundation stone for the new cathedral, the great building we have today; it is probable that Margaret was with him. A few weeks later he was dead, and one of their sons with him, killed in the Battle of Alnwick. His widow was to die before the year was out.

Her story strikes a contemporary note. A Saxon princess-in-exile, she was brought up in Hungary, and having come to England, was once again deported as a result of William the Conqueror's ruthless policies towards the Saxons, this time to Scotland. Malcolm took her in as an asylum-seeker and married her. She and her greatest son David, her successor to the throne, were perhaps the architects of medieval Scotland. Her piety, particularly her devotion to the Holy Trinity and to the cross, her energy for philanthropy, her support for the religious life, her investment in education, her care of the poor and her efforts to reform the Church were legendary even in her lifetime.

Kate Kellaway, writing in *The Observer*, says: 'The people in Paula Rego's paintings seem to know more about themselves than we can begin to grasp. The future is in their eyes, possessions and in their stillness' (7 November 2004). This describes her Margaret painting exactly. It shows her in her double bereavement, gazing into the far distance, as if her sights are already set on the next world. Her face is lined with the marks of suffering. Her hand rests upon her cherished gospel book. At her feet sits David, king-to-be, perhaps caught between the lure of the weapons lying like a child's toys around him, and the summons of his mother's gospel book to fight different, spiritual battles. Son and dying mother: a kind of *pietà* in reverse that echoes a sculpture nearby in the cathedral of the Virgin holding the body of her son. In a way, the themes are the same: a kingship not of this world, a vocation where royalty means walking a *via dolorosa*. It is not a comfortable painting, but then Margaret was not one to reign in comfort while others suffered. But the resolution, courage and resignation written in her face say something about how hard won are the civilizing Christian influences of learning, charity, justice and spirituality that she sought to instil in the people of Scotland. They were constantly at risk in a cruel age when poverty, disease and war meant that for most people life was nasty, brutish and short.

We can sum up these civilizing influences as wisdom. Margaret's far-sightedness is more than looking *beyond* the ordeals of this world towards the rewards of the next. She is as much looking *into* this world as a woman who, without losing her grip on what is required of an effective ruler, has nevertheless gained a larger perspective. Unusually for a ruler of her time, her power was not exercised at the expense of her subjects, nor was her privileged position abused in the pursuit of wealth and pleasure. Rather, her Christian wisdom gave her a view of things that enabled her to see the issues of her time for what they were. Her ultimate concern was the welfare of her kingdom and God's honour. For this reason, Dunfermline Abbey, which she founded and where she is buried, is one of the holy places of Scotland.

The ancient world knew well that wisdom was a prerequisite for leadership. In Plato's *Republic*, the author sets out a vision of a society that lives according to the noblest ideals of which human beings are capable. He sees his state ruled by philosopher-kings or 'guardians' who would lead the people into the knowledge of what is just, beautiful and good. Their role was more than simply to lead well: it was to embody and express the collective wisdom of the city-state. 'Until philosophers are kings . . . and wisdom and political leadership meet in the same man,' he says, 'cities will never cease from their evils – no, nor the human race, as, I believe – and then only will this our state have a possibility of life and behold the light of day' (*The Republic*, 473 c–d).

This called for personal qualities that Plato explores carefully. They include the ability to think rationally, to act with courage but also with generosity, to be disciplined, and to practise restraint in the management of the appetites. It is a highly polished, sophisticated vision of leadership in society that continues to have much to say to us in our own day. And while Plato comes from a classical tradition very different from the older Semitic world, his teaching has much in common with the insights of ancient Near Eastern wisdom. Egypt, Assyria, Babylon all had groups known as the 'wise' closely associated with the royal court. Their role was both to educate young men for high office in the nation, and to advise the king in his discharge of his responsibilities. At least in aspiration, wisdom and leadership are never far away from each other in antiquity.

Israel was no exception to this. Like her neighbours in the ancient Near East, the kingdom of Israel grew wisdom schools that proved highly influential in the intellectual development of her life and in the formation of the nation's leaders. Probably the model of the wise as educators and advisers under the patronage of the court was directly imitated from the surrounding cultures. Given that the court was increasingly cosmopolitan, with much trading and intellectual contact with other nations, it is not surprising that some of the Old Testament's wisdom writings turn out to be strongly influenced by those of Egypt and Babylon. Indeed, at least one whole section of an Old Testament text seems to have been lifted from an older Egyptian source without much alteration. And with the increasing influence and prestige of the wise came the desire to associate it with a great figure in Israel's history, just as Moses was seen as the patron of law, and David of the psalms. That great figure was Solomon.

In the Hebrew Bible, no fewer than three wisdom books are associated with Solomon: Proverbs, Ecclesiastes and the Song of Songs. The Apocrypha has another, the Wisdom of Solomon. Those ascriptions come from a time long after Solomon's reign when he had become a legend as the king who presided over Israel's golden age. There is more to Solomon's reign than his remembered glory, as we shall see in the next chapter. Yet we should notice the association of wisdom books with a royal figure. The tradition is telling us that the highest ideal of the good leader should be to become wise. What this means for the leader we shall see presently. The fundamental point is that the greatest blessing that can happen to any nation is more than material prosperity or freedom from war or natural disaster. What matters most is wise leadership. Of this, Solomon, despite his faults, was seen as the great exemplar.

Solomon, says the writer, 'loved the LORD, walking in the statutes of his father David' (1 Kings 3.3). He begins his reign in the best possible way, at prayer. God appears to him in a dream and asks what he should give him. What will he ask for? The usual suspects would be wealth, success, victory, to be well spoken of and to live a long time. Who could resist toying with gifts such as these? So the winsome simplicity of Solomon's request is both courageous and touching.

> I am only a little child; I do not know how to go out or come in. And your servant is in the midst of the people whom you have chosen, a great people, so numerous they cannot be numbered or counted. Give your servant therefore an understanding mind to govern your people, able to discern between good and evil; for who can govern this your great people? (1 Kings 3.7–9)

God is pleased with this, and promises not only the wisdom he has asked for, but also the requests he did not make: riches, honour, a long life. In these, as in his wisdom, says the Lord, no other king will be able to compare with Solomon.

A hermeneutic of suspicion might wonder whether Solomon is merely being clever here, second-guessing what God really wants him to ask for, and calculating that a place in history is earned by a quick-witted leader with an instinct for a spiritual sound-bite. Prayer has always been beset by the tendency to disguise self-interest as altruism, and ordinary human relationships are not exempt from it either. However, we don't need to deconstruct the text in this way. It presents us simply and beautifully with a man facing awesome responsibility and doing what we all must do at these defining moments of life: offering who and what we are to God, asking for wisdom and discernment without which Solomon knows, and we know, that we are lost. Indeed, the nature of the prayer itself demonstrates how wise Solomon is, for knowing what we do not know or don't possess is always a mark of personal insight. We shall see more than once in this book that self-knowledge is the basis of all true wisdom.

As the story unfolds, Solomon's gift of wisdom is presented in a number of guises. The first test, deciding between the two mothers both of whom claim the same child, demonstrates his ability to make sound judgements and make pastoral decisions with integrity. The evidence is decisive: 'They stood in awe of the king, because they perceived that the wisdom of God was in him, to execute justice' (1 Kings 3.28). There follows an extended account of Solomon's administration of the kingdom, the message being that wisdom is also about the practicalities of sound administration and effective stewardship (1 Kings 4.1–28). And wisdom is named as the origin of his creative gifts as a writer and composer as well as his unrivalled knowledge of the natural world (1 Kings 4.29–34). The writer's point is that the wise leader has insight into the nature of reality, including that part of it that is the human society of which, in Plato's word, he is the guardian.

It is a commonplace of the literature on leadership that a good leader understands complexity and has learned how to manage it. I shall explore later on how a good spiritual leader must not be afraid of complexity, whether it is the baffling complexity of the world in which we live or the complex human problems and dilemmas that are the daily stuff of pastoral ministry. But we should notice at this point how wisdom is focused on tasks that are the ordinary agendas of a nation's day-to-day life. In the Hebrew Bible wisdom means not only the inward attitude of integrity and understanding (the *why* question) but also competence and capability (the *how*). Solomon had an empire to oversee and a large court to run. There were alliances and trading relations to develop, an army to maintain and a temple to build. The highly organized, centralized state that Israel had become by the late tenth century BC was a world away from the modest coalition of tribes Saul inherited at the outset of the nation's life less than a century before. It is comparable to the difference between the common life of the first generation of Christians, and the emergence during the next century of a more organized expression of the Church led by monarchical bishops. This is an inevitable process. It results in a shift in leadership style away from the charismatic to the more institutional, something that is well documented both in the history of ancient Israel and of the early Christian Church. Saul headed an unstable confederacy of tribes. Solomon found himself at the head of an *institution* built to last.

This is an important point for those in ordained ministry. The roles of 'clergyperson', 'priest', 'deacon' or 'bishop' are formally assigned functions of the public ministry of the Church. This brings with it responsibility for an institution, whether it is a local church or parish, or an area such as a deanery or diocese. My observation is that this aspect of ordained ministry is not always understood or welcomed. Yet the development of Israel as an institution with a monarchy, temple and political structure was needed if the people of the covenant were to survive in the world to fulfil their calling. In a similar way, the Church has needed to go through the same evolution in order to become a society capable of realizing its vocation to bear witness to the kingdom of God. To understand how 'institution' is not inimical to 'mission' but can and should be its servant does require a leap of the imagination when 'institution' has become such a disparaged concept. In the same way, clergy need to reimagine the role of public representative of religion and see it, not as a hindrance to creative ministry but a tool given them for its delivery. The governance and care of the Church as the people of God ought not to be a burden but a privilege.

Unlike Solomon, clergy are not called to reign over anyone (though they may need to remind themselves of this from time to time). But they are called, like Solomon, to the privileged task of leadership. One of the major themes in this book is that ordained ministry is not a private response to God's call (we should always beware of the language of 'my' vocation as if it were somehow our own inalienable possession) but *the taking up of public office in the Church*. It is God who calls. 'Discernment' is a tripartite conversation between God, the individual and the Church. Once recognized, equipped and ordained, clergy are (whether or not they put it this way) the authorized representatives of organized religion in society, or to put it more theologically in Austin Farrer's striking phrase, 'walking sacraments' of the love and goodness and presence of God in the world.

Leadership in any organization these days is exacting, and especially so in the Church when our society holds such an uncertain attitude to religion. Many clergy find it difficult to hold their nerve when pushed to the margins of people's needs. Either they become consumed with self-doubt and begin to lack all conviction, or they compensate by believing in their own omni-competence, as if they can 'know the unknowable, solve the unsolvable and make reality go away' as Wesley Carr pungently puts it. Or they simply engage in displacement activity, doing any number of tasks that are not really part of the core calling of a minister of religion. There may be the enjoyable illusion of feeling more central to society's concerns, but it is always at the cost of realizing the possibilities of a crucial *religious* role.

I am not underestimating the difficulties of being ordained in western European society in the twenty-first century. But it's possible that we are not always accurate about these pressure points. Not all the tensions experienced by the ordained are due to a secular environment that has little time for Christianity, and the decline in church attendance and pressure on resources that are the result. The evidence of 2,000 years of church history is that ministry has always been the most demanding of callings. The scrutiny under which the New

Testament places the motives of those who offer their services to the Church illustrates this. The struggles of Jesus' disciples to do what was asked of them takes us back to the very beginnings of witness to the gospel. We can go further and reflect on the ministry of Jesus himself, from the ordeals of the wilderness to Gethsemane and the crucifixion. It is all of a piece with our own experience that to give our lives to the service of the gospel is the hardest task we can embrace.

To pray as Solomon does is to utter the natural cry of anyone summoned to an office for which he or she is barely ready. 'I am only a little child . . . Give your servant therefore an understanding mind.' In leadership, especially in the Church, we know in our heart of hearts that what we ask for at this defining moment will determine our entire history. So in asking God to equip us for this responsibility, what will we ask for? We can hope that most clergy on the eve of their ordination would not fall for the obvious siren voices of popularity or success, though the longing for fulfilment is perhaps more common and especially seductive in an age so obsessed with the meeting of personal needs. But other requests might also come to mind: the ability to preach well or to win many souls for Christ, or to be disciplined in prayer, or to make a difference to the injustices of society.

It is not wrong to have such ambitions at the outset of ministry, just as Solomon would not have been wrong to pray for the wealth that his court needed to be credible, or for a long life to complete his task, or for victory over his enemies. These were all arguably important for the task he was about to undertake. What goes into making a good preacher, a skilled pastor, a fervent evangelist, a man or woman of prayer, an advocate for social justice, are similarly important for clergy; and ultimately all these are God-given. But a new and qualitatively different way of being a king is needed if the practice of leadership is truly to model something of how God himself leads and governs his people. Solomon identifies this 'something more'. He recognizes that it is 'a wise and discerning mind'. He is given it, together with the other gifts he covets but does not ask for. In the Sermon on the Mount, exactly the same principle is applied to what we ask for in prayer. Jesus says that 'your heavenly Father knows that you need all these things. But strive first for the kingdom of God and his righteousness, and all these things will be given to you as well' (Matthew 6.32–33).

The issue is to raise our sights as high as God's. That is why Solomon's prayer is so remarkable. It comes from the heart of a king who sees himself as God sees him, not arrayed in splendour amid the panoply of power, but humbled and awed by what God is asking of him. That in itself is the divine gift Solomon covets. It has been given before he even opens his mouth. In the language of Augustine, God has already given what he commands, the wisdom to see and understand his own condition before God. It is the natural prayer of those called to lead. It belongs at the outset of ministry when, in the ordination service, the candidates both pray it for themselves publicly and are surrounded by the Church's prayer with and for them: 'Come, Holy Ghost, our souls inspire', *Veni Sancte Spiritus*. But the work of ministry is not simply begun in God, it is continued and ended in him too. All ministers who are trying to keep their vocation alive know that the longer they serve, the more they need to pray in the spirit of Solomon, and the more heartfelt their prayer becomes. To stop praying is to cease believing in God: it is probably as stark as that.

Napoleon said that 'a leader is a dealer in hope'. This is why ordained ministry exists: because ministers are called, like every Christian, to 'be ready to make your defence to anyone who demands from you an account of the hope that is in you' (1 Peter 3.15). In the kingdom of Israel, hopes were never higher than at the outset of Solomon's reign. As we shall see in the next chapter, they were destined to be disappointed – bitterly. Yet one greater than Solomon is now among us. He invites us to participate in his mission of love to humanity and to the whole creation. In a society that does not even know what its own longings and hungers are, to be a dealer in hope is a huge privilege and an awesome responsibility. How to present the hope of the gospel honestly, intelligently, attractively in our time calls for wisdom of the deepest kind. But wisdom, in the Hebrew sense of having insight into the way things are and where God is to be found in them, is itself the bearer of hope. For it gives direction, opens up possibilities, declares that nothing is beyond the capacity of the Creator to turn to his purposes of good. In that presence so full of promise and hope, Christian faith recognizes, celebrates and loves Christ, the power of God and the eternal wisdom of God.

2

The seductions of power: Solomon (Part 2)

In a charity shop some years ago, I picked up a small, dog-eared Victorian volume called *Time and Tide by Weare and Tyne: Twenty-Five Letters to a Working Man of Sunderland on the Laws of Work*. Installed as I was in a cathedral city on the River Wear (as it's usually spelled) a few miles upstream from Sunderland, I bought the book for a few pence. Its author was the great nineteenth-century writer John Ruskin. It is one of the most accessible of his works, a distillation of his best thinking on the social condition of England in his day. The book has much to say about public life, the economy, religion, the nature of work and the ethics of trade. The subject of the thirteenth letter is 'Episcopacy and Dukedom' in which he explores what it means to exercise leadership and oversight. He has a striking insight about a familiar word:

> There is, I suppose, no word which men are prouder of the right to attach to their names, or more envious of others who bear it . . . than the word 'noble'. Do you know what it originally meant, and always, in the right use of it, means? It means a 'known' person; one who has risen far enough above others to draw men's eyes to him, and to be known (honourably) for such and such an one. 'Ignoble', on the other hand, is derived from the same root as the word 'ignorance'. It means an unknown, inglorious person. And no more singular follies have been committed

by weak human creatures than those which have been
caused by the instinct, pure and simple, of escaping from
this obscurity. Instinct, which corrupted, will hesitate at
no means, good or evil, of satisfying itself with notoriety
– instinct, nevertheless, which, like all other natural ones,
has a true and pure purpose, and ought always in a
worthy way to be satisfied. All men ought to be in this
sense 'noble'; known of each other, and desiring to be
known. And the first law which a nation, desiring to
conquer all the devices of the Father of Lies, should
establish among its people, is that they *shall* be so known.
(John Ruskin, *Time and Tide*,
London: George Allen, 1897, p. 74)

We can assume that the poor working man of Sunderland had
not considered the etymology of the word, but I had not considered it either. The root is *gnosis*, of course, but the word has
evidently undergone a lot of elaboration in its long history.
That what we now think of as *noble* – greatness of mind and
character, of high ideals, dignified, large-hearted, generous –
should have something to do with being *known*, is thought-
provoking.

On reading Ruskin, my thoughts turned first, not in the
direction he intended, but towards a building his reader
would have known well, the cathedral I serve as a dean. I often
use the word 'noble' to describe Durham Cathedral. Everyone
with a feeling for history, architecture and spirituality agrees
that Durham Cathedral embodies the very finest to have
come out of the English Middle Ages. To a remarkable degree,
the cathedral expresses the highest possible vision of life as
the Christian gospel understands it before God: its incomparable setting above its wooded loop of the River Wear, its
pioneering Norman architecture, the proportion and balance
of its interior spaces and that elusive quality of spiritual

'presence' so connected to the humble saint in whose honour the cathedral was first built and whose shrine it contains, Cuthbert. All this and much more goes into the virtuosity that makes the cathedral a building that is not only beautiful but truly *noble* in Ruskin's sense of being 'known' for the things that make it loved.

Yet there is another side to the building. It was begun in the year 1093 in the aftermath of the Norman Conquest. In the north of England, William the Conqueror's ruthless subjugation of the Saxons, known as the 'harrying of the north', was a recent and bitter memory, an act of what we would now call ethnic cleansing that had cost many lives. William's successor, Rufus, proved to be no less cruel than his father had been. It was during his reign that Norman hegemony in the north was consolidated. The symbol of power in old Northumbria was Durham Cathedral, perched strategically on its fortified peninsula next to the castle. The message could not be clearer. England's new rulers were there by divine appointment. The cathedral was an explicit symbol of Norman political power. As such, it stands as evidence of how noble aspiration is deeply compromised by hubris.

How the building of a church plays out the tension between spirituality and pride is the theme of William Golding's novel *The Spire* – as it is, in a more racy and popular vein, of Ken Follett's *Pillars of the Earth*. Both books explore how human ambition is inseparable from spiritual vision. To do something great for God seems incapable of being disentangled from doing something great for ourselves. This is as true when we 'build' in a mission sense, through church planting or growth for instance, as when we build with bricks and mortar. I want to explore in this chapter how we negotiate this pitfall faced by all leaders. But perhaps Durham Cathedral can help us learn a first lesson straight away. It is that nothing is gained by denying the facts. The cathedral is what it is as a matter of history. That it would have been experienced by many native people as oppressive is not up for debate. So the spiritual question is, how can a great but compromised vision ✕ be reclaimed for the kingdom of God?

Perhaps (if I can be allowed to use this kind of language), Durham Cathedral holds several keys to its own redemption. One of them is in the shrines of Cuthbert and Bede, two saints for whom nothing mattered save the honour of God and the salvation of the world. The simplicity of their tombs set within the magnificence of the cathedral draws the starkest, most eloquent contrast between hubris and humility, a constant reminder to cathedral clergy not to think more highly of ourselves than we ought to think. Another is the life of the community that inhabited the building over the centuries and continues to do so today. To say that 'church' is people and not simply a building is a commonplace so frequently trotted out that it has become a cliché. For all that, the truth still needs to be lived out if a cathedral, or any church, is to have a human face. But the ultimate 'sign of contradiction' in this and every Christian church is the cross of Jesus. The cross is the visual focus to which all perspectives lead; the symbol of dying to ourselves in the power of the One who laid down his life for his friends. It gives the building its purpose and provides the clue to how it is to be read, whatever the conscious or unconscious intentions of those who built it. If Durham Cathedral is a *noble* building, the only nobility that ultimately counts is that which the cross gives it.

The church building is an apt metaphor of ordained ministry because both the building and its leadership are visible signs of an institution dedicated to the public proclamation of faith. In the Old Testament, the exemplar of this is Solomon. As we have already seen, he was remembered by the Bible as the patron of wisdom. But he was also remembered as the king who presided over Israel's empire when it was at its most extensive and glorious. The symbol of this golden age was the temple that he built. It represented the promised reign of peace and plenty that God had promised his righteous king and his fortunate subjects. For Solomon and his successors, the fortunes of the nation were largely associated with the temple. Indeed, the king probably had a key ceremonial role in an autumn festival celebrated each year in it, so that his own identity was largely fused with that of the sacred place of which he was regarded as the guardian. This is why, in the later prophets, the corruptions of both institutions, monarchy and temple, were seen as aspects of the same fundamental disease.

We can trace this tension between spirituality and pride particularly clearly in the career of Solomon. His story is a case study of the choices leaders constantly face. We shall see later on how the book of Proverbs, probably intended to instruct young men in the arts of leadership, pictures a youth on the threshold of adulthood walking down the street. Two voices call out to him, inviting him to listen to what they have to offer: Lady Wisdom and Dame Folly. They symbolize the battle that takes place endlessly for a person's soul; indeed, the battle that takes place *within* it. The theme of the two ways – truth and falsehood, wisdom and folly, righteousness and wickedness – is common throughout wisdom literature. There is a sense in which we are always standing at a cross-roads with a choice to make.

Solomon epitomizes this divided self. Even at the outset of his reign which started so well, there is an undertow of ambiguity and compromise in the text. Before his accession, the story hints at his possible complicity in the palace intrigues that led to his becoming king. As soon as the text has told us that the kingdom has been 'established in the hand of Solomon' (1 Kings 2.46), it straight away informs us that he has made a marriage alliance with Pharaoh, and moreover that the shrines at the high places have not been removed

(3.1–2) – both points of which the Deuteronomic writer is severely critical. And even the account of the achievement he was most to be remembered for, building the temple at Jerusalem, is interrupted by a passage about his other major building project, the construction of his own palace. It tells us that he spent almost twice as long on the king's house as he did on the Lord's house (6.38; 7.1), an interesting comment on the shifting of Solomon's priorities and a hint of the self-aggrandizement that was to prove Solomon's fatal flaw.

It comes to a head with the eleventh chapter of 1 Kings where Solomon's continued alliances with foreign women lead to such far-reaching religious compromises that the text concludes that 'Solomon did what was evil in the sight of the LORD [YHWH], and did not completely follow the LORD [YHWH], as his father David had done'. This is a devastating indictment from a writer who earlier spoke so glowingly about Solomon's wisdom and love of God. As we shall see, David's own career was itself sufficiently compromised by his inability to manage his personal relationships that it is to some extent a case of 'like father, like son'. The difference seems to be that whereas David's flaws stemmed from his inner personal complexity, Solomon's were more related to what psychoanalysts call 'grandiosity'. This is the unconscious or semi-conscious acting out of the delusion that we are gods, capable of doing anything. It is a reversal of how the leader and the institution are intended to be to each other. Instead of serving and empowering others, leaders who are prone to grandiosity regard their institution as their personal possession, existing for the sake of their own needs and agendas. This is why institutional power is intoxicating: it plays into the tendency of omnipotence.

Buddhists speak of being 'single-pointed', devoted only to the spiritual centre of the human being, undistracted by the 'noise' of all the competing claims on us that cry out for our attention. Kierkegaard spoke about 'the truth for which we must live and die'. The story of Solomon is not only the dissipation of hope in disappointment or the collapse of vision and corruption through power: it is the loss of purity, the abandonment of the very quality for which he had been so commended that the story finds so distressing. And the consequences did not end with Solomon. His ever more tyrannous use of power and his merciless imposition of tax-ation on his subjects heaped up hostility and resentment in the kingdom, especially in the north where the tribes had felt more loosely connected to the centre at Jerusalem than in the south. When Solomon died, his kingdom split in two, irrevocably. It was the tragic end to a glorious era. The responsibility can squarely be laid at his feet.

There are two points here. The first is to do with what appears to have gone wrong in Solomon's exercise of his role. It seems a classic case of the corrupting effect of power: the king progressively separating himself from his people through the erection of magnificent buildings, complex administrative systems and armies of servants, slaves and concubines. No doubt dynastic kingship in the ancient world required this elaborate machinery to be credible. It was how monarchy functioned: wealth, display, command-and-control, myriads of sexual partners, all went into bolstering the public image of the king, signalling the potency of a nation and symbolizing the favour of its gods. Yet it's a long way from the humble origins of David his father keeping his sheep, who for all his faults never forgot his calling to be a shepherd of his people. The institution has travelled a long way in just a generation, and not to the benefit of the people. How far the warnings of Samuel the prophet about the oppressive character of monarchy had proved right when he said: 'In that day you will cry out because of your king, whom you have chosen for yourselves; but the LORD will not answer you in that day' (1 Samuel 8.18).

This is a problem for all those who are the official representatives of organized religion. Deacons, priests and bishops stand at the visible apex of a public institution, the Church. It is a position of real power: not economic or political power so much as symbolic, spiritual power. We need to learn how to exercise power wisely and responsibly; that is to say, for the good of those we serve. If we fail to learn this, we shall not only damage other people and harm the institution we are part of, but also put at risk our own selves.

It was captured for me when a priest from South Africa visited Durham Cathedral recently. He joined us for prayer, when we had the pleasure of meeting him. Later, he spoke to a colleague about his experience. He said that the sheer immensity of the cathedral and its spiritual power had led him to expect that the Dean would be someone of 'very great stature'. He meant it in an ironic way: cathedral clergy must necessarily be tall enough for their scalps to scrape the vault. We smiled; yet it left me pondering. Was my personal, intellectual, spiritual stature as a priest under scrutiny here? What do we mean by 'stature', and how do we 'stand' as ministers? The temptation is to stand as tall as we can so that we fill the institution we lead. Yet Jesus says that true greatness means becoming like a little child. This suggests that true 'standing' means *not* filling the space ourselves but making room for others. While the clergy represent the Church publicly, they are not themselves the Church. Vocation does not mean 'going into the Church'; it means responding to the call to lead and serve in such a way that the Church becomes more truly itself, the body of Christ the servant bearing witness to his grace and truth.

Wisdom means practising humility in the spirit of the Servant of the Lord who 'did not regard equality with God as something to be exploited, but emptied himself, taking the form of a slave' (Philippians 2.5–11). Ministry must always be lived according to this kenotic way of self-emptying, remembering it is to become servants of *God's* way of wisdom, which St Paul says is the foolishness of the cross. It means keeping close to those we minister to, not allowing the ordained role to put distance between us and our fellow human beings who are also fellow members of the baptized community. It is easy in public ministry to think we are something, and to lose touch with the reality of why we are here at all.

My second point is this. Our beginnings in life are always shot through with hope and expectancy, and rightly so: setting out on marriage, the forging of a new friendship, the birth of our children, a new house and home, a change of job, and of course ordination. As we undertake this awesome rite of passage and emerge with the new role of deacon, priest or bishop, the whole community stands alongside in solidarity and support to wish and pray for us every gift, every blessing, every happiness that God has to give. I was ordained deacon and then priest more than 30 years ago, and the glowing memory of those days and the sense of being strengthened by the liturgy, and by the prayer and support of family, friends and community has never left me.

But wisdom has to do with seeing beyond the early successful stages of leadership into the more tricky later phases when we have to learn about our own fallibility, how to say sorry, mend relationships, live with our mistakes and their unintended consequences. Perhaps it is unkind to suggest to a newly ordained man or woman that they will ever make mistakes in the future, and that some of them may be costly. Yet a clear memory of one of my ordination retreats was my personal interview with the bishop. He said to me: 'Michael, in your ministry, despite your best intentions, you will get things wrong sometimes, you will hurt people, you will fall below the standards God sets for you and you set for yourself. *When* that happens, not *if*, you need to claim the forgiveness of Jesus, pick yourself up, mend what you can and carry on. That is the grace and the miracle of Christian ministry.' I have not forgotten the words, and I have not forgotten the kind and gentle way in which they were spoken, as if – and I can't know this – they came not out of some theory but out of his lived experience.

Of course, he was right. There have been failures in my own experience of ordained ministry that it is hard with hindsight to have to own up to. John Henry Newman said that 'to live is to change, and to live long is to have changed much'. Part of this change, when it is happening in a healthy, God-given way, is the process the New Testament calls *metanoia*, the change of mind and heart that comes from realizing the truth about ourselves, seeing the past for what it is. Our English word for it is 'repentance'. It is hard enough to repent when we have wilfully acted against what we know to be right. It is harder still when unconscious forces have acted upon us unnoticed, unrecognized, until some symptom has drawn attention to an unheralded spiritual danger. Of these, the cancer of institutional power is one of the most hazardous in any leadership role, but especially in ordained ministry. It amounts to the sin of pride. At these hardest of times in ministry, I have needed to remember gratefully what a wise bishop once said to me.

But the falls of ministry are potentially a source of wisdom. Like the fall in the garden of Eden, there can be, by grace, an element of *felix culpa* about our mistakes, for in the sometimes bitter experience of having failed lie the seeds of wisdom. In Marcel Proust's series of novels that make up his great reflective work *A la Recherche du Temps Perdu* (*Remembrance of Things Past*), he meditates on his own past and tries to find a way of remembering that is not hopeless and unforgiving:

There is no man . . . however wise, who has not at some period of his youth said things, or lived a life, the memory of which is so unpleasant to him that he would gladly expunge it. And yet he ought not entirely to regret it, because he cannot be certain that he has indeed become a wise man . . . unless he has passed through all the fatuous or unwholesome incarnations by which that ultimate stage must be preceded . . . We do not receive wisdom, we must discover it for ourselves after a journey through the wilderness which no-one else can make for us, which no-one can spare us, for our wisdom is the point of view, from which we come at last to regard the world . . . We must not repudiate [the past], for it is proof that we have really lived.

Perhaps it is telling that Solomon's prayer at the dedication of the temple includes a surprising petition: 'O hear in heaven your dwelling-place; heed and forgive' (1 Kings 8.30). To recognize that the prayer for forgiveness belongs to *foresight* as well as to *hindsight* marks the high point of Solomon's *insight*. It is noble to pray in this way, aware that even the best that we offer is fallible and always falls short. In the Lord's Prayer, the clause 'forgive us our sins, as we forgive those who sin against us' has a future reference as well as a past and present one, for its focus is the coming of God's kingdom. This is why, when I speak to ordinands on the threshold of their public ministry, I suggest that the prayer for wisdom should include the prayer for forgiveness when they lapse from it. Its source is not only realism about our human condition: it comes out of deep thankfulness for the limitless mercy and forbearance of God, and that the cross which we proclaim to others is also the endless source of our own forgiveness and reconciliation.

The washing of feet is increasingly being associated with ordination, either as part of the rite itself, or as a more informal act during the retreat. It is a beautiful and poignant symbol of renewing the offering of life in ministry, understanding the origins of that in the service of others. But that action is not simply to imitate what Jesus did in the upper room before his Passion: it is a symbol of what Jesus continues to do for his friends. In the beautiful words of Archbishop Michael Ramsey, we should pray that he will 'serve us often, serve us daily in washing our motives, our ambitions, our actions', so that we always serve others in the costly way he has loved and served us. This is the meaning Christianity gives to what it is to be 'noble', for it is Christ's way of being known.

3

An interpreter abroad: Joseph

Clergy do not often preach on weekdays. But on two occasions in recent years, weekday sermons have presented challenges that have been among the most demanding I have had to face in the pulpit.

The first was on a Tuesday evening one September. At the time, I worked at Sheffield Cathedral. The bishop had arranged a service there to license ministers to various responsibilities. The day before, I had written an upbeat, even humorous, sermon based on the film *Chocolat*, which chronicles the nefarious goings-on around a *chocolaterie* in a remote Burgundian village. The theme was that delight in God is at the heart of ministry, and that joy is the best witness to the gospel of Jesus Christ. I had worked and refined the text carefully (there would be a large audience) and I was looking forward to preaching. At lunchtime the next day, television images flashed across the ocean told the world that something terrible had happened in the United States. It took only minutes to realize that it would not be a matter of rewriting my sermon but preparing an entirely new one. I said in my address that those ministers would never forget that they had begun their new ministries on 11 September 2001.

The second occasion was a Thursday evening in March. It was St Cuthbert's Day, one of the greatest days of the year in Durham Cathedral which has been his shrine for more than 1,000 years. It was the day fixed for my installation as Dean:

what better day to begin a ministry in Durham? I had, again with great care, crafted an address around St Cuthbert and the power of his life to speak to the concerns of men and women in the twenty-first century. Because cathedral installations involve a lot of preparation and rehearsal, and because I needed to greet family and friends who had travelled north to be present, I had written my sermon several days earlier. I should have known better: it's a mistake in ministry to be too prepared too soon. Once more, world events took over and set their own agenda. All week, the talk was of war on terror, and of an imminent invasion of Iraq. On the day itself, 20 March 2003, invasion looked increasingly likely, but it was not yet certain. I listened to the news throughout the day and rewrote the text hour by hour. Just before the service began, it was confirmed that the allied invasion had been launched. By then I was out of time, and had to resort to a kind of homiletic brinkmanship and hope that the words would come out right.

All clergy will have had similar experiences when what they have carefully scripted is overtaken by unexpected events in the world, the nation or the local community. The task at times like these is to try to say something that will connect with the bewildered thoughts and chaotic feelings of those gathered in church. If the expectation on the preacher is to deliver the word of God into human situations, then it is an inescapable requirement to respond from the pulpit to this wish for connection. To do anything else, or to do it glibly, would be unforgivable. My experience tells me that what I have been doing, albeit fallibly, has been to try to *interpret* what is happening, attempt to offer a preliminary reading of events in the light of faith in the God whom the congregation has gathered to worship. This is absolutely *not* to provide answers to tragedy. But it is to suggest how faith 'bears witness' to suffering, shapes a response even in the immediate aftermath of tragedy, and begins to articulate it. We shall return to these points in the chapter on Job.

The science or art of interpretation, much prized by the wise in Israel, is the theme of this chapter. Interpretation lies at the heart of wisdom, for in its many manifestations, wisdom is always a way of looking at reality that finds *patterns, connections* and *meanings*. As we shall discover later on, biblical wisdom is shot through with the vocabulary and imagery of 'seeing'. Having 'insight', 'perception' or 'illumination' are among the gifts that characterize the wise who 'see' in ways that casual observers fail to do. Wordsworth, in a beautiful phrase in his 'Lines Composed a Few Miles above Tintern Abbey', talks about 'seeing into the life of things'. That is a way of speaking that the biblical writers would have recognized.

This works at many different levels, all of them important in the Hebrew Bible. In a practical way (and common sense was much prized by the wise of Israel), it can mean skill, capability, competence, a sound economic head, prudence, good management – lessons we have seen drawn from Solomon's success. It can mean knowing how the world functions, understanding the laws of nature, cause and effect, what in the West was once called 'natural philosophy' – and philosophy, of course, is literally the love of *sophia*, wisdom. It can mean going beneath the surface of things, understanding deeper meanings: qualities like insight, discernment and awareness. This includes understanding and learning from history, emulating the good and avoiding the bad. It can mean the ability to make music and write poetry and proverbs, for which, again as we have seen, Solomon was famed. It can mean having a properly developed moral compass, knowing good from evil and right from wrong, and not simply knowing this but living according to it. It can mean detachment from fear, acquisitiveness and envy, an inward stability of character. In all this, the wisdom writers stressed the importance not only of understanding for its own sake, but also of training the young to understand in their turn. Education, *paideia*, is how the values of each generation are transmitted to the next, and this has always been of paramount concern to the wise of every civilization.

At its heart, however, wisdom is a *religious* quality. In the book of Job, there is an interlude in the middle of a speech by Job defending his innocence. It's a song that poses a question. What is the most valuable resource in creation, infinitely more precious than gold, silver or precious stones, or anything else that can be mined in the depth of the earth? The answer is: wisdom. Nothing is more valuable than wisdom, and only God knows its origin. Yet it is accessible to mortals as what he both requires and gives. 'The fear of the Lord, that is wisdom; and to depart from evil is understanding' (Job 28.28). Elsewhere it's spoken of as committing our way to the Lord, trusting in him, walking in the good and safe paths of righteousness. The wise man or woman is someone who knows where they belong in the scheme of things. It begins with God's well-ordered world in which everything has its place and purpose. It expands to include a human being's relationship with God the Creator, the source of wisdom, and Wisdom itself. Archbishop Michael Ramsey used to speak about 'the dignity of creaturehood'. The wise practise a piety that flows from recognizing what is due to almighty God, and offering life as a continuous act of worship.

Understanding this, say the wisdom writers, is to begin to discern God's way with the world and with human beings. The Hebrew Bible tells a number of stories that seem particularly designed to explore not only how God works mysteriously through the lives and histories of people and nations, but how there are people gifted with insight who can see into the meaning of events and understand the patterns hidden within them. The Court History of King David (2 Samuel 9—20; 1 Kings 1—2), the stories of Daniel and his friends (Daniel 1—6), the Joseph narrative (Genesis 37—50) all have this character. In each of them, the role of wisdom is made much of, to the extent that you could call them 'enacted' or 'narrative wisdom', novella-type commentaries on 'taught' wisdom books like Proverbs.

In its structure and its vivid depiction of human character, the Joseph story is one of the most perfect narratives not just in scripture but in human literature. At the outset of the tale, young Joseph, his father's favourite, is the envy of his brothers and is portrayed as not altogether wise in how he handles his relationship with them. After drawing back from their original plan to murder him, they sell him as a slave, and he comes to Egypt where his common sense and managerial skill earn him a senior position in Potiphar's household. A crude (and failed) attempt at seduction by Potiphar's wife lands him in jail, where he demonstrates his childhood ability to interpret dreams. Restored to high office in Pharaoh's court, he sets about organizing Egypt in readiness for the coming famine. So successful is he that people across the Near East come knocking at Egypt's doors for supplies of grain, among them his own brothers. The recognition scene in which he and they are reconciled is one of the most moving episodes in the Bible.

One of the purposes of the story is to portray Joseph as a wise man. He demonstrates shrewdness as a manager in Potiphar's house, in prison and then over all Egypt. He negotiates the politics of nation and court with skill. He behaves with integrity when compromised by a seductress. He knows what is required in a crisis such as the years of famine. He has respect for his father, and he has compassion for his brothers. What is more, the story is not afraid to show him weeping at times: wisdom, it seems, means not simply prudence and piety but also emotional intelligence.

But more than anything else, we see Joseph as a man with the gift of interpretation. In his youth he has his own dreams and sees far-reaching significance in them. Other people tell him theirs: the butler, the baker, Pharaoh himself, and he under-

An interpreter abroad: Joseph

stands their meaning. He can discern what God is doing or is about to do, and counsel a proper response. At the climax of the story, following his reconciliation with his brothers, he discloses that he is even able to understand the mysterious workings of providence and read the meaning of events within the larger purposes of God. 'Even though you intended to do harm to me, God intended it for good, in order to preserve a numerous people, as he is doing today. So have no fear' (Genesis 50.20–21).

The interpreter is a pregnant image of the ordained minister. A primary task of ministry must always be to help people understand what God is doing in their lives and in the world. I have spoken already about pointing to meanings, and uncovering significance, not simply human significance (though that matters), but supremely, *divine* significance. Of course, to talk of meaning at all in a postmodern age is a daring act of faith. In the ancient world, no one seriously doubted that providence, dreams, omens, sacred texts all carried meaning; the only question was, *what* meaning? Today, when there is suspicion of 'grand narratives' we have to step back, like Qoheleth the preacher in Ecclesiastes, and ask the more fundamental question: how do we discern pattern, structure and connection in the world, and what kind of language is needed to speak about it to our contemporaries? Before we even open our mouths, we the ordained are a paradoxical sign of an older way of reading reality that is largely alien to many people in the West today.

We establish meaning in many different ways. We do it as preachers and evangelists, where we bring the life-changing power of the gospel to bear upon human life and experience. We do it in the celebration of the liturgy, where we play at living the kingdom life, as if it were already fully present; and as Augustine said, we see the mystery of our own selves upon the altar, transformed as part of God's new creation. We do it in our pastoral care of individuals, when we attempt to read the

43

stories of people's lives in the light of the value God puts upon each one of them as created in his image and loved for ever in Christ. We do it in our social engagement, by putting the questions and challenges of the kingdom to situations where justice and mercy are unacknowledged or forgotten. All this is about discerning 'divine significance' as God's interpreters.

The interpreter is, if we like, God's spy in recognizing and naming falsehood, deception and illusion for what they are. In John Bunyan's *The Pilgrim's Progress*, Christian comes with his heavy burden into the house of the Interpreter. As he steps inside, he is shown a painting. It shows a man 'with his eyes lift up to heaven, the best of Books in his hand, and the Law of Truth writ on his lips; it is to show thee that his work is to know and unfold dark things to sinners, even as also thou seest him stand as if he pleaded with men'. This man, says the Interpreter, is the guide that Christian must follow on his journey. It is of course a portrait of Christ, depicted as both travelling companion and destination, the interpreter *par excellence* of our pilgrimage. In knowing and unfolding dark things and standing 'as if he pleaded with men', he is the model and exemplar of what we are. For the incarnation of the Word is God's final and decisive act of interpretation by which his movement towards us is revealed as grace and truth. John Calvin says near the beginning of his *Institutes* that the function of the scriptures is to give us spectacles through which the world comes into focus. We could describe our task as interpreters in the same way: to bring reality into focus, *God's* focus. When Christian leaves the house of the Interpreter, he sees where he has to go. He comes to the wall of salvation and finds the cross, where the burden he has carried for so long falls off his shoulders, and he is free.

The work of interpretation comes down to being a *theologian*. Theology gets a bad press these days. Politicians talk disparagingly about not getting embroiled in the 'theology' of a particular issue, when they mean arcane logic-chopping as opposed to practical action. Many clergy and lay people admit to not being 'theologians', meaning that they are not bookish or academic. One important way of rescuing the word is to say that the whole Church is a theological community, because it exists to testify to its origins in the redemptive love and mercy of God. So as soon as any baptized person bears witness to his or her faith or utters a prayer or recites the creed in worship, that person is immediately 'doing' theology. When the Church gathers to celebrate the Eucharist or pray the daily office, it is demonstrating its theological character.

In a more technical sense, however, 'theology' is what we do when we reflect on the world and on our own human existence in the light of faith in God. To do this requires knowledge of the faith tradition, especially of the scriptures and how they have been understood down the centuries. The trusted public role of the clergy in preaching, presiding at worship and exercising pastoral care requires them to be trained and equipped as theologians who can speak for the Church. There is a necessary intellectual component to being a good theologian in this 'professional' way of seeing it. The intelligence Joseph shows in the story is not only emotional and spiritual, but also theological. This is of a piece with wisdom as an intellectual movement in Israel that not only seems to have had a particular concern for the education of the young, but sought to make theologically intelligent practitioners out of all who held leadership positions in the royal court and in the nation as a whole.

To be a public theologian and interpreter is undoubtedly a great and daunting responsibility. Every time we open our mouth we risk misunderstanding the scriptures, misinterpreting the tradition, misreading what God is saying and doing, and misleading those whom we serve, perhaps dangerously. Abraham Lincoln said that it is better to keep your mouth

shut and be thought a fool than to open it and have it confirmed. We know we are fallible: this, too, wisdom teaches us.
But there are God-given ways by which we are kept close to
the mind and heart of God and learn to read his ways.
We shall look at some of them in a later chapter: the old-
fashioned disciplines that shape ministerial character and
nurture the inner life, like daily prayer, immersion in the
scriptures, frequent attendance at Holy Communion, regular
spiritual direction to help us know ourselves and test out our
perceptions. We should add to that our own theological and
spiritual formation through reading, study, a programme of
ministerial development, and not least, as I shall also say later
on, enriching our 'hinterland' through literature, poetry, film,
music, the arts – all of them so often the unlooked-for sources
of wisdom and insight in our time.

But if interpretation is a responsibility that should make us
tremble, it is also one of the joys of ministry. The story says
that Joseph 'reassured' his brothers, 'speaking kindly to them'.
To 'reassure' people by helping them glimpse how, in the
changes and chances of the world, love is his meaning is a
privileged theological task. To say, 'The Lord meant it for
good', is not to warble some glib formula that covers up our
inability to say anything meaningful (as when, following a
tragic death, people resort to clichés such as that it was
'meant' or 'God's will' or 'for the best'). Nor does it come from
some desperate craving for a happy ending, the closure that
makes everything all right again. It comes out of the profound
theological conviction that the cross and resurrection of
Christ have transformed the world by overturning the death-
dealing powers that oppressed it. It comes from the consequence St Paul draws from the gospel, which is to ask, 'If God
is for us, who is against us? He who did not withhold his own
Son, but gave him up for all of us, will he not with him also
give us everything else?' (Romans 8.31–32).

We saw in our study of Solomon that the business of leadership is hope. Ministry is to be a practitioner of this, for if the Church is looked to for anything by those who care about life, it is as the bringer of hope. By being skilled and sensitive interpreters and theologians, alive to the complex realities of life, clergy help turn back the tides of despair that threaten to engulf so many today. Ministers ought not to be grandiose about this project hope. It is rarely that a piece of oratory or writing dramatically turns a situation round by its large-scale impact on hearts and minds. More usually, it happens in small, intimate settings where a parish congregation, a local community or individual men and women find, to their surprise and delight, a reorientation in life that is truly God-given and transformative. In the Middle Ages, theology was regarded as the queen of sciences. If so, then it shows its royal pedigree by its humility, its contentment not to be over-ambitious, its willingness to wash feet. In this, it emulates the way of being royal lived out by its subject, Jesus crucified and risen. The medium and the message are one.

There is one further insight that wisdom imparts to the task of interpretation. The classic path of mystical theology commends, as both the starting- and the end-point, the practice of silent contemplation. Sometimes we have said all there is to say, and we must simply weep God's tears of compassion with those who suffer, or delight with him in all that is good and happy in life. If there is nothing to say, at least not yet, we must not be afraid of the theology that is done without words. St Francis is supposed to have told his brothers: 'Preach the gospel. Use words if necessary.' The philosopher Ludwig Wittgenstein said: 'Before that whereof we cannot speak, we must be silent.' In Israel, to know when to keep silence is always a mark of the wise, for this gives space for God himself to speak. As William Cowper's great hymn says, 'God is his own interpreter, and he will make it plain.'

4

A young man in exile: Daniel

Nothing perhaps so typifies the dislocation of the modern world as the plight of refugees and asylum-seekers. There is something especially poignant about those who are not only without a home, but also without a place to call a homeland. Whether they are technically 'stateless' because their country of origin has disowned them, like the Ugandan Asians of the 1970s, or have come to the bitter realization that their nation is no longer a safe place in which to continue to live, the experience is the same. Like those who have been bereaved (for that is precisely what in some ways refugees are), people who are undergoing this trauma describe an entire range of emotions: loss, bewilderment, disorientation, isolation, anger, longing, searching, and even failure and guilt. The past, of course, features strongly, whether it is viewed as gone for ever and unrecoverable, or whether there is a belief that to some extent it can be reconstructed in order to give shape to an uncertain and frightening future.

The experience of exile is not unique to the Jewish people, but it has been a recurrent theme in their history. My mother's family belonged to the comfortably off, well-educated, liberal Jewish community in the Rhineland of Germany. Like most German Jews of the 1930s, they regarded the rise of the Nazi party as an aberration, a fit of madness that would soon be over once the German people saw sense. If you had asked many Jews of that period how they described themselves, they

48

would have said that they were proud to be German. Their menfolk had served the Kaiser in the Great War and been honoured for it. Their contribution to the economic recovery of Germany after the war had been outstanding. They celebrated the great legacy of German learning, culture and art. Among Jewish families, Luther, Dürer, Bach, Beethoven, Goethe, Schiller and Kant were proud household names.

As the decade advanced, it became clear that the German Jewish community was in great danger. Parents hastily made arrangements for their children to be sent to safe places abroad. Great Britain took in 10,000 Jewish children through the celebrated *Kindertransport*. Many of them would never see their families again. The anguished farewells at railway stations, their utter bewilderment on arriving in England, their varied fortunes under the roofs of British families are movingly chronicled in the film *Into the Arms of Strangers*. In it, survivors tell what it was like to be refugees. Identity looms large in their stories: who am I now, what shall I become, how do I survive this? Some of those interviewed in the film have said of their experience, in effect, 'Once an exile, always an exile.' Their children, the so-called 'second generation survivors', often have a strange sense of belonging yet not belonging, even in the places that have been 'home' all their lives.

What we call the Exile is a, perhaps *the*, defining experience of the Old Testament. In 587 BC, Judah was finally overrun by invading Babylonians. Jerusalem was razed to the ground, the temple destroyed, and much of the population, including the nation's leaders, deported to Babylon. It marked the end of an era that had begun with the founding of the monarchy five centuries before at the time of Saul and David. At a stroke, the exiles found themselves without a king and without a temple; that is to say, without any way of organizing their common life and practising their faith. More fundamentally, the Exile raised agonizing questions about their covenant with God. He had said that they would be his people, and he would be their God. They were to know and obey him in the land he had promised to give them. Where did the covenant stand now? Where was God in the disaster that had overtaken them? Was there any meaning in the history they were going through? Their cry of disorientation is echoed by all who have lost everything and wonder if they have a future: 'How shall we sing the LORD's song in a strange land?' (Psalm 137.4, AV).

It is not a question without an answer. Some of the most profound texts of the Old Testament reveal the seriousness with which people of faith began to wrestle with what it meant to be in exile and learn to discern the presence of God in a new and alien environment. The historians, prophets and poets of the Hebrew Bible testify to how rich and creative this time of exile would prove to be when it came to probing more deeply the mysterious acts of God. Despite the hardship and suffering of exile, it proved, paradoxically, to be a gift. It taught the Jewish community that God was not to be confined to particular places or particular institutions such as they had known before. He was to be understood as infinitely larger, more mysterious, more wonderful in his dealings not simply with the Jewish people but with all people. His concerns were nothing less than universal. Historians of religion agree that it was during this period that monotheism, the belief in a single, supreme deity, became the unambiguous faith of Israel. So when the exiles returned to their land three generations later, they were a very different community from the one that left it.

I believe that the Exile offers a telling image of the state of religion in modern times. In western Europe, organized religion has been in free-fall since the 1960s, and despite endless mission initiatives and 'fresh expressions' of church life, all fuelled by the incurable optimism (and sometimes denial) of church leaders, there are no signs that the tide is turning.

Telling this truth is extraordinarily difficult: bishops don't like to think of themselves as presiding over a dwindling institution and managing decline. It is no argument to point to the growth that is taking place in some areas of church life, the inventiveness of many ordained and lay leaders these days, or the deepening of spiritual experience that is happening in many places. These are indeed welcome and God-given; but they are not, for now at any rate, able to withstand the relentless undertow of what the poet Matthew Arnold famously called the sea of faith's 'melancholy, long, withdrawing roar'. Today's worshippers and their ministers are strangers to their contemporaries who neither understand nor care what Christian faith has to say to the world. Nowadays, it is not that twenty-first-century men and women have forgotten what they once knew: they never knew it to begin with. We are a people in a strange land. We are exiles.

How do we, as ministers, sing the Lord's song in a strange land?

Among the many texts of the Hebrew Bible that tackle this question is the book of Daniel. It purports to tell how Daniel and three other Jewish young men are brought to the Babylonian court to be educated. There they face various ordeals designed to test their faith and their loyalty to God's covenant. It begins simply enough with the young men refusing to eat the rich food and drink set before them, preferring a simple diet of vegetables and water as a sign of their distinctiveness in an alien environment (Daniel 1.8ff.) The three are then arraigned before Nebuchadnezzar for failing to worship the golden image that he has set up. For this they are thrown into a burning fiery furnace. However, they emerge unscathed, delivered by a mysterious fourth figure with 'the appearance of a god' (Daniel 3). In a similar story, Daniel is condemned for praying to his God YHWH and not to the king. He is thrown into the lions' den; but once again, God's protection ensures that he is unharmed (Daniel 6). The message is clear: the faithful are vindicated, an example and inspiration to all who are suffering persecution. And this exactly meets the situation out of which this book was probably written, the fierce persecution of the Jews by the Hellenistic ruler Antiochus IV 'Epiphanes' in the middle of the second century BC.

Like Joseph, Daniel demonstrates the ability to hold on to his integrity in a pagan court. Like him, Daniel is elevated to a position of trust, though not without severe testing on the way. These stories of faithfulness to God are one example of the character of Daniel who is introduced at the outset, together with his friends, as 'versed in every branch of wisdom, endowed with knowledge and insight, and competent to serve in the king's palace' (Daniel 1.4). And like Joseph, Daniel's wisdom is demonstrated specifically in his ability to interpret dreams and understand visions, both his own and those of others. He explains Nebuchadnezzar's two dreams of catastrophe: one that is coming upon his kingdom (chapter 2), the other that is coming upon himself (chapter 4). He alone can read the ominous writing on the wall at Belshazzar's feast (chapter 5). This prepares us for the second half of the book, which is devoted to Daniel's own visions of the future (7—12). 'Apocalyptic' means 'unveiling', and the intention of these visions, written, like the court stories, for people undergoing persecution, is to disclose God's future purposes of good for the faithful, and to reassure them that no human authority is more powerful than the kingdom of God whose reign will ultimately prevail. The message is that since Daniel has demonstrated his wisdom in his ability to interpret the dreams of kings, the interpretation of his own visions can be safely trusted.

At first sight, both the stories and the visions of this book suggest an attitude of implacable hostility to Babylon on the part of Daniel and his friends. They are under the constant assaults of an alien cultural, intellectual, theological and spiritual environment. This extends all the way from the intimate and personal to the public and political, and it forces Daniel to face the issue of his own integrity. You don't do business with the gods, kings and customs of Babylon: you stand out against them. Not to do so would be to compromise your witness and collude with idolatry. And while the stories of Daniel have something of a deceptively simple morality tale about them, the visions in the second half of the book leave us in no doubt as to the seriousness of the life-choices they depict. In the visions, the coming kingdom of the Most High smashes in pieces the pitiful world empires in their self-aggrandizement and claims to the ultimate loyalty of their subjects. It is the 'one like a son of man coming with the clouds of heaven' (7.13), who has 'dominion and glory and kingship'. His reign will never pass away.

How to preserve identity 'in a strange land' is a pressure on religious leaders that is felt particularly keenly, for they are the public representatives of their faith and their deity. They embody its values, preside over its ceremonies, articulate its content and answer for its meaning. So when a faith community is at odds with its environment, its leaders are inevitably in the front line of a controversy that can feel like the clash of civilizations. In the West, the leaders of all faiths are under pressure to adapt, modify and reinvent their ancient traditions in the light of secular modernity. The tensions between 'conservative' and 'liberal' are visible everywhere in Islam, Judaism and Christianity, sometimes dangerously so. These tensions get played out locally in a thousand different ways. Religious leaders are constantly faced by choices that come down to those illustrated in the stories of Daniel. Their role is to preserve and promote the distinctive identity of their faith. Yet they are perceived to be as strange to the world as that world is strange to them. What does it mean to be 'wise' when faith is either not understood, or is even actively opposed?

An obvious answer to that question, and a right one, is to point to Daniel's unswerving obedience to God and loyalty to his covenant. He is depicted as the man who has been formed so firmly in his faith that when the time of trial comes, he has within him the resources to face it and be vindicated. It's an obvious point to make to those who lead the Church today, but it cannot be said too often that our 'formation' as followers of Jesus is the foundation on which all of ministry is constructed. The rock on which we build the house of ministry is familiar and well tried. It is no new insight to say that public ministry is based on the knowledge of the scriptures and the tradition in which we stand, together with the rule of prayer, meditation, sacrament and study by which we order our life – themes we shall return to in a later chapter. This alone is the source both of public credibility in ordained ministry and of our confidence in practising it. Daniel's stand for faith is presented as an act of real courage. It's the fruit of a lifetime's personal and spiritual investment.

Something like this seems to lie at the heart of Jesus' schooling of the disciples in the upper room as he prepares them for his Passion. 'If the world hates you,' he says, 'be aware that it hated me before it hated you. If you belonged to the world, the world would love you as its own. Because you do not belong to the world, but I have chosen you out of the world – therefore the world hates you' (John 15.18–19). For St John, the 'world' represents all that stands in opposition to the grace of God by refusing to 'know' him (John 1.10). In that Gospel, the choice to stand in the world or in God is presented as the stark decision between darkness and light, death and life: there is a cosmic drama being acted out in which human beings must take sides. So the upper room is a place of shaping and character-building where the disciples – those who will lead the Church in the future – are taught about the necessity of abiding in Christ, growing in mutual love, bearing fruit in his service, practising prayer. These are the marks of faithfulness and the evidence of true discipleship. They are required of those who are fit to face the world, live in the world, bear witness to the world, but not, in John's language, to 'belong' to the world.

The sharp delineation of 'Church' and 'world' that this implies is not easy for many twenty-first-century Christians to contemplate, especially not for clergy, who inevitably find themselves negotiating an uncomfortable and problematic 'edge' as visible symbols of one kind of world in the midst of another. The difficulty is in knowing what this boundary is meant to represent. There are pressures both within and outside the Church to construe it in terms simply of taking positions, whether on women's ordination, or issues of personal ethics such as abortion, euthanasia and, especially, homosexuality. I am not pretending that these are not important issues. But they can be pretexts for easy (even lazy) speeches that rehearse established positions without leading to an intelligent or serious conversation either between the Church and the world, or between Christians who differ. I doubt if these will turn out in the long term to be defining issues about the fundamentals of faith such as the book of Daniel addresses: the nature of the true God and the worship due to him rather than to idols, even if many people *do* construe these ethical debates as first-order matters. But wisdom means a reflective 'take' on who and what we are in the context in which we live; so it has to mean understanding what is, and what is not, of enduring significance for religion.

The book of Daniel can help us here. In their encounter with a culture that is strange and threatening, the exiles are forced back on to the core values by which they live. This comes down to one thing only: their adherence to the loyal worship of YHWH. It is all they have. It is not inconceivable that they might have renounced the worship of YHWH in favour of idols. The young men are not sure whether the God whom they serve can deliver them from the furnace (Daniel 3.17–18); and when it is Daniel's turn, it's the king, not he, who holds out the forlorn hope that his God may after all deliver him (Daniel 6.16). But there is in these men the spirit of the early Christian martyr Polycarp who famously said, before being thrown to the lions, 'For 86 years I have served him, and he has never done me wrong. How can I now blaspheme my King who saved me?'

I have suggested that in the stories of Daniel, wisdom means developing a secure religious *identity*. Thomas Carlyle was restating an old insight from the classical world when he said that people become like the gods they serve. We are formed by what we give our lives to: this is how our identity is conferred and the centre of our selves shaped. To worship idols, in the language of the Bible, is the displacement activity that happens when we cease to acknowledge the claims of the Creator upon us, and worship the creature rather than the Creator, as St Paul puts it (Romans 1.25). Put like that, it's clear that in the 'strange land' of our secularized twenty-first century, the idolatries of power, cruelty, addiction, greed and lust are successfully forming people in their own image. In this environment, Christian witness remains as urgent as it always was: to live out with conviction yet with courtesy the more excellent way of love in imitation of the self-giving love of the God who was in Christ reconciling the world to himself. For this cruciform identity is the saving heart of the new and more generous way of living that is Christianity. It is wisdom's answer to the powers that oppress and diminish us. Where everything is at risk of breaking up, this centre holds, for it is love's response to the creative and redemptive love of God forever at work in his world.

If the very existence of the world is love's project and love's work, and if Christian ministry is to be a living symbol of this way of love, can there be any negotiation with the 'world' as the place of negativity and threat? In the second part of this book, we shall see how wisdom takes a larger view than simply regarding the world as an insidious and dangerous place. Some texts stand back from the flux of life and question its fairness, asking whether there is any purpose programmed into the universe. Others affirm it as the sphere of God's creative activity and a place of pleasure and play. It is true that the world-affirming influences of wisdom were darkened in apocalyptic books like Daniel by the experience of savage persecution. If the world is perceived as hostile and threatening, that is hardly surprising in the circumstances.

Yet there are glimpses of another view of the 'world' in these stories. The picture we get of Daniel and his friends is not of people cut off from those with whom exile has brought them into an unlooked-for contact. They were educated in 'the literature and language of the Chaldeans' (Daniel 1.4), and there is no hint, in a book that might be expected to provide it, that this immersion in the culture of Babylon is unwelcome. As if there were any doubt about this, the book suddenly abandons Hebrew halfway through the fourth verse of chapter 2 and continues in Aramaic, the native language of Babylon, for a further six chapters. This is telling, given the significance the Hebrew language had acquired by the time the book was written as a clear marker of Jewishness. When not directly attacked for their faith, the young men's relationships with those who move in the royal court are co-operative, even cordial. Daniel and his friends quickly earn respect and trust in this strange land, and this paves the way for Daniel's privileged access to the king as an interpreter of dreams whose wisdom the native magicians cannot match.

This seems to offer a model of how a positive relationship with the world is compatible with a convinced religious identity. Indeed, perhaps we could say that it is *required* by it. Far from resulting in a withdrawal from history and a passivity in the face of crisis (a trait apocalyptic writers are often accused of), Daniel and his friends demonstrate a way of being engaged that is entirely true to the wisdom traditions of their faith. I like the phrase 'critical friendship' to describe this relationship. 'Critical' implies not buying into the assumptions on which life lived beyond the direct influence of wholesome religious faith is based. It allows for space to have a prophetic engagement with the prevailing *mores* of a society and its leaders, confronting in a way that can be uncomfortable and demanding. To be 'critical' means to make a judgement, and this requires a proper degree of detachment in order to see things as they really are. This is where a well-formed, secure Christian identity is crucial. Yet 'friendship' suggests a presumption of sympathy, of walking alongside, listening, asking questions, lending understanding, support and care. Those whose attitudes and behaviour come under scrutiny are our fellow human beings, flesh of our flesh; their propensity to be seduced into the endemic idolatries of our age is no different from our own. *Hypocrite lecteur, mon semblable, mon frère!* wrote Voltaire: we are all the same, and the dilemmas we face in this and every age are common to us all.

We began this chapter by asking the question of exile: 'How shall we sing the Lord's song in a strange land?' It is the task of leadership in exile to help a community answer that question. The stories of Daniel suggest the qualities such leadership is going to need if it is to be effective in our own century. The text sums it up in the words 'wisdom and understanding', allied to an unbounded confidence in God and his purposes for the world. And while the stories do not offer us grounds for thinking that there are easy escape routes from the intractable complexities of living in exile, they are nevertheless undergirded by the hope that the world has not been abandoned to its fate. Kings see the error of their ways and become wise by acknowledging the most high God. Daniel and his friends are honoured by their oppressors for remaining faithful. There are signs of reversal and transformation. This is what sustains us in Christian ministry. We should look for those signs and celebrate them. The book is courageous enough to ascribe to Nebuchadnezzar his own *Magnificat* as he belatedly honours the King of heaven: 'all his works are truth, and his ways are justice; and he is able to bring low those who walk in pride' (Daniel 4.37). We could say that to bring the world to sing *Magnificat* is what Christian mission is for. As we sing the Lord's song, the land of our exile becomes a little less strange. It may even begin to feel like home.

5

Private faces in public places:
David

———⇒•⇐———

On the morning after I was installed as Dean of Durham, I was wandering round the cathedral to get a feel for the building and to meet some of the people – visitors, worshippers, paid staff and volunteers – who were there that day. As I walked up the south quire aisle, I came across a young stonemason who was busy carving an inscription of some kind on a tablet on the wall. With something of a frisson, I saw that what he was carving in the stone with infinite care and concentration was my own name. I was the latest entry in the long list of the priors and deans of Durham that went back to the year 1083. Others were watching, and it was a source of amused interest that there was just enough room to include my own name on the tablet. After that, space would have run out. Could this mean, we speculated frivolously, that I was destined to be the last of the deans, and that the office would become extinct once I had gone, or that the end of the world would happen during my incumbency?

It was odd to see my own name appear out of stone and realize that I had become a small part of the fabric of the building. In a church such as Durham Cathedral, it was impossible not to be humbled by this, not to feel the awesomeness of the responsibility that had been laid upon me the previous evening. At the same time, there was a certain absurdity about it. After only 12 hours in office, I was already all but immortalized. Never mind what the coming years would bring with their potential for doing good or ill, never mind how history would judge my tenure of the deanery, at least my name would live on as long as the cathedral was still standing. I might turn out to be wise or foolish, intelligent or stupid, courageous or cowardly: none of this would affect the fact that my name was now permanently inscribed as a part of the fabric of the place I had come to serve. And of course, this was not because of who 'Michael Sadgrove' happened to be in the early years of the third millennium, only that he held office in a particular place at a particular time. That alone earned my place in the family tree.

That we are remembered matters considerably. But *how* we are remembered matters much more. In the annals of Israel, no leader was better loved than David. He was gratefully remembered as the king who had fought with giants and completed the conquest of Canaan. He was looked back to as the father of the nation. He gave it secure borders and earned for it a respect among its fellow nations it had never had before. He founded a dynasty that endured – no mean feat in the ancient world. But his personal qualities were remembered as much as his political achievements. His spirituality was fervent and committed, as the ascription of so many of the psalms to him suggests. 'In all that he did he gave thanks to the Holy One, the Most High, proclaiming his glory; he sang praise with all his heart, and he loved his Maker' (Ecclesiasticus 47.8). In the memory of Israel, he set the standard by which all other kings were judged. So far was his reign regarded as a golden age that as longing grew for the coming of a messianic king who would bring in God's reign of peace and plenty, it was in words and images drawn from the story of David that this great hope came to be expressed.

In the light of how later tradition looked back to the glories of David's achievement, it is all the more striking that one of the primary, and earliest, sources for his life takes a far more ambivalent view of his career. It is found in 2 Samuel 9—20 and 1 Kings 1—2. Like the story of Joseph, it is one of the most vivid narratives of the Old Testament, beautifully crafted and with an attention to plot and character that mark it out as among the greatest literature to come out of the ancient world. Why was it written? At one level, it seems to have been told in order to show how David's throne was finally secured for Solomon and his descendants. It links the false start, as it sees it, of Saul's failed attempts at kingship, and the success of the dynasty through the line of Solomon that follows it. Perhaps it was written by someone close to the royal court who wanted to celebrate the monarchy as God's gift to Israel. What is intriguing about the narrative is that, from start to finish, it is not obvious how things will turn out. The story skilfully explores how court politics, personal relationships and personality traits combine to create an environment so unstable that it is not certain whether David will even *have* a throne to bequeath to a successor. So after a narrative in which the reader can feel at the mercy of cross-currents pulling this way and that, it is a relief to reach solid ground with the conclusion that 'the kingdom was established in the hand of Solomon' (1 Kings 2.46). At last, the God-given direction has been found.

Like the storyteller who gave us the Joseph narrative, this author has remarkable insights into the various ways in which people negotiate life. The story of David offers more 'enacted wisdom' that draws lessons from the career of its key protagonist. The author wants to make sure, of course, that David is remembered. But this is not the usual stuff of royal hagiography that tells of the heroic battlefield successes and noble deeds for which the king is loved by his subjects. Indeed, this writer seems to go out of his way to avoid the courtly style with its easy flattery that characterizes most writing about royalty from that day to this. Instead, his interest is in how David's career illustrates a universal truth about public life, that the *leader* and the *human being* belong inextricably together. To summarize a subtle and complex story, he seems to be saying that the public and private lives of a leader are a single whole. You cannot have a good monarch without a good person underneath; and if the person underneath is flawed, their flaws will inevitably work their way out into public visibility, often with spectacular and damaging consequences.

After a few preliminaries, the narrative cuts to the chase with the episode of David's adultery with Bathsheba (2 Samuel 11). The sight of a beautiful body on a neighbour's roof, the fantasy and the acting out are dwelt on less than its terrible consequences. David, aided and abetted by the fiercely loyal Joab, hatches an elaborate plot to eliminate the wronged husband by sending him into the thick of battle where he is most likely to be killed. The message is: 'Do not let this matter trouble you, for the sword devours now one and now another' (2 Samuel 11.25). As soon as it is decently possible, David takes Bathsheba as his own wife. No comment is passed among his subjects about this calculated and cruel act. Perhaps some shrugged it off as an entirely normal act of *force majeure*; others may have said that what a leader does in his or her private life is not anyone else's business provided the public performance is not affected. 'Don't see, don't tell.'

But the storyteller, with real sophistication, is at pains to tell that this is not some momentary aberration on David's part. There is, he says, a basic fault in his psyche, an inner dislocation that insists on playing itself out until tragedy ensues before the gaze of an entire nation. The next episode concerns David's children (2 Samuel 13). One of his sons, Amnon, is in love with the sister of half-brother Absalom. Like his father on his roof-top, Amnon's passion for Tamar torments him. So a cunning plot is devised to make their union happen; and incredibly, David colludes with it, either because he is blind to what is going on before his very eyes, or (what is worse) out

63

of weakness to please his son. The deed becomes known, and Tamar is ruined. Yet David refuses to punish Amnon 'because he loved him, for he was his firstborn' (2 Samuel 13.21). So Absalom takes matters into his own hands and avenges Tamar by killing Amnon. He flees from his father who takes no action other than to mourn the loss of another son. Soon, Absalom is fomenting rebellion against David, with the result that David himself is forced into temporary exile. Eventually, Absalom is found and killed, and David returns to his throne a chastened and weakened man. Things are never the same after that. In later years, says the narrator, he becomes sexually impotent, a metaphor of his waning political authority. One more pretender tries to seize the throne; only just in time does David summon up the strength to name Solomon as his heir.

The wisdom literature of the Old Testament could be said to be driven by a single concern, which is the well ordering of life. Its appeal to human beings who would be something and do something with their lives is to take their cue from the created world in its beauty and order. We have already seen in Solomon's career how life-choices beckon the leader at every turn. To choose, or be seduced by, foolishness is to be pulled into a chaotic existence without principles, disciplines or norms. To embrace wisdom, on the other hand, is to live according to the pattern and structure that are embedded within the creation and within *us*, to be true to our God-given nature as creatures who reflect the good order of the Creator. We shall see later on how the young man in Proverbs, called to make the choice between wisdom and folly, is a leader in the making, someone who inhabits court circles and is particularly susceptible to the corruptions of power and privilege. The story of David might well have been intended as a parable of leadership in crisis. It's a warning to leaders of what happens when inner demons can no longer be contained. Then everyone is victim.

There is no substitute for reading this marvellous story with its acute psychological understanding of the life of a great but flawed leader. I want to draw from it two insights that I believe are important for anyone in public life, but especially for those in the ordained ministry.

The first is the observation the story unambiguously makes that what we are in our personal lives and relationships is inextricably linked to what we are in our public lives and leadership roles. It is a fallacy to imagine that it doesn't matter what we do or are in private provided our ministry is unaffected. For one thing, personal integrity cannot be compartmentalized. If we are not trustworthy in one area of life, every other aspect of our selves must be at risk. This is not a popular doctrine with politicians who fiercely defend themselves in the face of financial or sexual scandal by saying that while they may 'regret' mistakes they have made (not least the mistake of being found out), the public's trust in them was never misplaced. This is not to condone the prurience of the tabloid press but to say that the public are right to believe the best of those who are accountable to them as their elected or spiritual representatives. They are right to expect consistency of motive and behaviour as much in personal life as in public office. When that belief turns out not to have been justified, something honourable has been subverted. Belief in the leadership has been disappointed, and the ideals for which it stood inevitably compromised. The lustre of 'nobility', in Ruskin's sense of being *known*, has been tarnished.

The consequences for public ministry of fracture in our personal lives are real and severe. This is not simply a matter of the reputational risk the Church runs when one of its leaders is found to have been engaged in what the canon lawyers call 'conduct unbecoming'. The inward drives and motivations that lead to wrong or inappropriate behaviour in private are not somehow switched off in public. They are still there, consciously or (more likely) unconsciously, colouring attitudes, affecting decisions, distorting the relationships that belong to ministry. We 'know' in the pulpit and at the altar what we are in our own 'room of pictures', as Ezekiel puts it, and at the best of times that dissonance can be disconcerting. And every minister is aware of how the high (and only true) motive in ministry of seeking the best for others can become subtly eroded by the hunger to meet personal needs of various kinds. The Church is littered with the human debris of those on whom clergy, in trusted positions of spiritual and organ-izational power, worked out their own self-regarding agendas. The story of David is just such a tale.

Towards the end of the New Testament period, much thought was being given to the shape of Christian ministry and its role in safeguarding the content of the gospel proc-lamation so that it could be handed on intact to successive generations. Out of this, in the second century there emerged a stable understanding of the place of ordination in the Church that has proved remarkably enduring. We might think that such a process would focus on the institutional forms of the ministry – how bishops, presbyters and deacons fitted into the structure of the catholic Church. But it's strik-ing how much emphasis is placed on the inward character of the ministry, and the qualities required of those who are to be ordained. In the Pastoral Epistles, as they are aptly called, this is the *sine qua non* of effective leadership. Here is just one example. The bishop (for which read anyone who has over-sight in the Church) must be 'above reproach, married only once, temperate, sensible, respectable, hospitable, an apt teacher, not a drunkard, not violent but gentle, not quarrel-some, and not a lover of money. He must manage his own household well . . . for if someone does not know how to manage his own household, how can he take care of God's church?' (1 Timothy 3.2–5). Later on, the author charges his young reader to 'pay close attention to yourself and to your teaching' (1 Timothy 4.16). This dual attention to what we are in our own selves as well as what we practise in our public roles is of a piece with Hebrew wisdom. Once decouple those things, and ministry will quickly unravel.

This points to the need for a true *spirituality for ministry*, and this is the second insight from the story of David. Following the affair with Bathsheba, and David's despatch of her wronged husband, the episode seems to be at an end, with David's reputation intact. Bathsheba mourns, and in due course David brings her home as his wife. It's unfortunate, but it has happened. The best thing now is to achieve 'closure'. So we might think. But here the narrative takes an unexpected turn. This is the appearance of a key character who has not been mentioned very much in the story up to now. That character is YHWH. 'The thing that David had done displeased the LORD' (2 Samuel 11.27). Wisdom narrative tends to be reticent about divine intervention into human affairs, both here and in the Joseph story. God's presence is understood to be implicit in human affairs, his providence working its purposes through the changes and chances of history. So the sudden and explicit introduction of YHWH into the narrative makes for an entrance of considerable dramatic power. This is sustained in the powerful dialogue that follows between the hapless king and Nathan the prophet whom God has sent to arraign him for his callous abuse of office.

The point is simple and obvious. What is veiled from human sight and knowledge is not veiled from the sight and knowledge of God. We may pretend that it is, and if we do, it is one more of the collusions we implicate ourselves in to protect ourselves from reality. We could call this 'functional atheism', the conscious decision to act as if there were not a God to whom we are accountable, or at any rate a deity who is concerned with the affairs of humans. 'The fool hath said in his heart: There is no God' (Psalm 14.1, BCP). This can be very selective and compartmentalized: David, we can be sure, never ceased to be a fervent and committed worshipper of YHWH; yet at one crucial point in his psyche there appears to have been a disconnection or fracture that put everything else at risk. I spoke earlier about the need to establish consistency between the inner and outer worlds of our existence, but the truth is that it is more complicated than that, for even being *inwardly* consistent is a challenge that is sometimes too hard to bear.

So a spirituality for ministry must have at its heart the relentless pursuit of inner transparency and integrity. The psalm that later became associated with David's repentance after his adultery puts it matchlessly: 'You desire truth in the inward being; therefore teach me wisdom in my secret heart' (Psalm 51.6). The implication is that what we need here we cannot attain by ourselves. An Augustinian theology of human life says that we are helpless on our own: only divine grace can give us what we lack. An Augustinian theology of ministry enfolds that fundamental fact of our human condition into its prayer for divine empowerment for the tasks of leadership. This is why ordination takes place within the setting of the Eucharist. It is only through God's gift of himself in Christ that human life can be released to achieve authenticity, generosity and truth; and it is only through the same gift that those qual-ities of transformed human living can be expressed in ministry.

It is in this spirit that we make our approach to the Eucharist. 'Almighty God, unto whom all hearts be open, all desires known, and from whom no secrets are hid: Cleanse the thoughts of our hearts by the inspiration of thy Holy Spirit, that we may perfectly love thee, and worthily magnify thy holy Name' (BCP). We know this beautiful prayer as the 'Collect for Purity'. That word has an old-fashioned, perhaps even repellent ring about it, not least because it has been largely hitched to the cause of sexual abstinence among the young, especially in conservative far-right churches. But we should not focus especially on this negative sense of being free from contamination. In the Sermon on the Mount, the word is used in a more profound sense as characteristic of a whole way of life. Those who are focused on the coming of God's kingdom embody this quality: 'Happy are the pure in heart; they will see God' (Matthew 5.8, GNB). To see God is the ultimate aim of living. To help others see God is the ultimate aim of ministry. To become pure in heart is therefore an inescapable requirement on all who are leaders in the Church. Without it, all ministry is fatally compromised.

I am suggesting that a spirituality for ministry needs to be centred on purity of heart. What does this mean? Kierkegaard said that 'purity of heart is to will one thing'. He meant that the pure heart is undistracted by the competing claims for ultimate loyalty that are made upon every human life. It is wholly given to the 'one thing' of seeing, knowing and living for God, making the offering of life its ultimate aim and purpose. The career of David shows how even the most committed leaders can fail, and when they do, their failures can affect the lives and destinies of many others. Failure in ministry is costly, painful and hard to recover from. Sometimes its damaging effects can be felt for a lifetime, in those who have been harmed by it and in ministers themselves. Yet in its vivid realism, and especially in its unpitying exposure of David's flaws, the story is not pessimistic. On the contrary, David is presented to us as the leader who gains the self-knowledge and the courage to acknowledge the truth about himself and find both forgiveness and strength for the future. The fact that the story concludes with the dynasty safely established is not so much a happy ending as the writer's celebration of the providence of God always at work in human affairs, mostly in hidden ways but always benignly.

Yet we should not miss the sense of release and new possibility that accompanies the words of Nathan to David: 'The LORD has put away your sin; you shall not die' (2 Samuel 12.13). The message is: life can begin again, and ministry too. If, as we have seen, the priest is a 'walking sacrament' of God's presence, then he or she is a walking sacrament of the healing power of forgiveness and grace in human life with all its flaws and failures. This means knowing our own brokenness in ministry. It is the theme of one of Paul's greatest letters, where he candidly sets out his understanding of himself as he perseveres in the task of bearing witness to the gospel. 'But we have this treasure in clay jars, so that it may be made clear that this extraordinary power belongs to God and does not come from us' (2 Corinthians 4.7).

What we are in ourselves is provisional and mortal. 'I preach as never sure to preach again, and as a dying man to dying men', as the great seventeenth-century Puritan minister Richard Baxter put it. But mortality does not have the last word. In the resurrection, the 'deaths' we experience can be transformed and swallowed up in victory; every 'end' can be a potential beginning. In his suffering and hardship, and, we can also say, as a man 'ransomed, healed, restored, forgiven', Paul is sustained by the hope of an 'eternal weight of glory' (2 Corinthians 4.17). Christian ministry doesn't simply utter words and perform actions that speak of life. The minister is a living testimony to the life-changing power of God. Our flesh and blood is not a perfect witness. But if our own faith and hope are a lived experience, our testimony will be 'good enough'. This is how David was remembered. When every other achievement is forgotten, perhaps it is not wrong to pray that we too may be remembered in that way.

Part Two

LEARNING FROM WISDOM

6

Wisdom and folly: the book of Proverbs

<hr style="width:20%" />

There is a science fiction short story called 'Nightfall' by Isaac Asimov. In it he pictures life on planet Lagash. It is a strange place. Historians of Lagash have learned that periodically, something catastrophic happens to life here. Several civilizations have flourished on the planet, but none of them has lasted more than 3,000 years. Then a global disaster takes place. Civilization reverts to a primitive state of existence and the cycle begins all over again.

In the story, we're coming up to the end of another 3,000-year cycle. Science and technology are highly evolved (again), and astronomers have learned that the planet is part of a system of six suns. The physics of this is complicated, but all we need to know is that these six suns orbit round one another in such a way that one or more of them is always in the sky at any time. So it's never dark on Lagash. Or almost never. Once every 3,000 years, when only one of these suns is alone in the sky, an invisible but very large moon passes in front of it and causes a total eclipse. This plunges the planet into darkness, not just for minutes but for several hours. And when the historians and astronomers start talking to each other, they realize that these periods of darkness correspond exactly to the times when civilizations hit a crisis and die.

There is a powerful religious cult on Lagash that keeps alive a curious myth. According to its followers, there are in the sky thousands, millions of points of light called *stars*. They are invisible, of course, because the sky is always lit up. So thinking people don't believe in stars, for there is absolutely no evidence that they exist. But according to the myth, every 3,000 years, when the world goes dark, an awesome sight appears, terrifying in its beauty. It is the epiphany in the sky of a myriad of stars: some constellated into shapes you could almost imagine to be animals and human beings; others in vast galaxies that march across the heavens like highways of milky light. And so awful is the darkness and so magnificent are the stars that people are driven out of their minds. To keep the darkness at bay and shut out the starry firmament, they burn everything they can: belongings, houses, cities, forests, anything to create light and keep sane. But the darkness and the stars always win. Everyone goes mad. Society reverts to its most primitive state, and then, when the suns come out again (for they always do), civilization begins its long upward climb until the stars show themselves once more.

It's all about what we see and what we don't see. The language of seeing and the light we see by provides an entire vocabulary of wisdom: words like 'insight', 'illumination', 'vision', 'disclosure', 'imagination', 'enlightenment', 'discernment' are among the metaphors that pervade the way all civilizations have spoken about wisdom. Biblical wisdom speaks about turning aside from the path of truth as a failure to *see*. Lagash-like, the 'big' truth is collapsed down to what can be comfortably managed within the confines of what is familiar, known and tested, a sort of two-dimensional projection of a three-dimensional reality. What people could not *see* they did not believe existed. Only religion on Lagash kept alive the memory of that 'bigger' dimension of the stars. But the sudden exposure to reality was too much to bear. Overwhelmed by the darkness and the stars, the people went mad.

Up to now, we have looked at some of the best-known stories in the Old Testament that have been influenced by 'wisdom', and asked what light these character studies shed on the practice of ministry today. A common theme running through them is how the wise person understands the larger context within which life is lived. Solomon at his best, Joseph and Daniel are its exemplars. By contrast, folly is not to know, or to forget, the true dimension of human living and to behave as if the only reality were what sight and sense portrayed, like David and Solomon in their later years. We could say that ordained ministry exists to testify to the 'stars', and to the conviction that darkness will not extinguish life and light. In the fourth Gospel, the incarnation of the Word is spoken of as light shining in the darkness, 'and the darkness did not overcome it' (John 1.5). To have 'seen his glory' and to testify to it is what we mean by Christian witness. To do this publicly is the specific calling of the ordained.

In the second part of this book, I want to explore these themes of 'seeing' and 'understanding' in the books of the Hebrew Bible we call 'wisdom literature'. Those classic texts are the books of Job, Proverbs, Ecclesiastes and the Song of Solomon (and in the Apocrypha, though we shall not be considering them here, the Wisdom of Solomon, and Ben Sirach or Ecclesiasticus). Folded into the wisdom books in our English Bible is the book of Psalms, and this includes a number of what some scholars see as wisdom poems, two of which we shall look at. In these books, Israel's thinkers wrestle with some of the profoundest issues of the human condition: the problem of pain, the unfairness of life, the search for meaning, establishing order in a chaotic world, the mystery of happiness. If religion has nothing to say about these things, then it has nothing to say – this seems to be what drives the writers of these great texts in their relentless pursuit of truth. The question for the clergy is, what do we have to say about these? What *insight* do we bring from what we have glimpsed of the 'stars'?

The book of Proverbs is one of the most polished texts in the Old Testament. Its aim is to instruct the young for adult life, perhaps for the service of the royal court. The opening nine chapters are a series of elegant poems in which various speakers vie for attention and compete for the soul of a young man. How is this youth going to be initiated into the ways of the grown-up world? His parents are first on the scene: 'Hear, my child, your father's instruction, and do not reject your mother's teaching' (Proverbs 1.8). 'Piety', in the ancient world, meant a sense of duty and obligation towards those who provide protection and care, and to whom respect is owed: parents, teachers, rulers, benefactors, the aged, the experienced, and ultimately God himself. It meant listening, learning and obeying. There is a great deal in the wisdom literature about the importance of transmitting values to the young, making sure that the wisdom of one generation is not lost in the next. High on the list of values that form the basis for the good life are loyalty, justice, truthfulness, not trusting in your own limited insight, having faith in God.

This is vividly spelled out in the image of two contrasting figures calling out to the young man as he walks down the street (Proverbs 9). Both are women. One is what the Hebrew Bible calls the 'strange woman'. She is described variously as a seducer and an adulteress waiting to entice the naive unwary youth with her promise of instant gratification. She is loud and ignorant. '"You who are simple, turn in here!" And to those without sense she says, "Stolen water is sweet, and bread eaten in secret is pleasant"' (9.13–18). This woman is more than a symbol of sexual licence: she is a personification of all that distracts human beings into waywardness. To enter her house is to be seduced not just by a specific temptation to wrong behaviour, but more generically, to become enmeshed in the trap of foolishness and adopt it as a way of life. This is Dame Folly. To fall for her, says Proverbs, is to go like an ox to the slaughter or to rush like a bird into the snare. It is a place of spectres and skeletons. 'They do not know that the dead are there, that her guests are in the depths of Sheol.'

Her opposite is the lady who beckons with a very different invitation. She too wants to entice the youth, but into a way of living that is wholesome, joyous and good. Her house is built on its seven pillars, her table set ready to welcome her guests; her invitation is to everyone who tramps the streets of her town. It exactly echoes that of Dame Folly: '"You that are simple, turn in here!" And to those without sense she says, "Come, eat of my bread and drink of the wine I have mixed. Lay aside immaturity, and live, and walk in the way of insight"' (9.1–6). The words are the same but not the same: stolen water across the street, mixed wine here. And while the simple and those without sense are simply confirmed in their actions by the very act of crossing Dame Folly's threshold, here the simple are made wise and those without sense are given insight. Dame Folly is a pantomime parody of Lady Wisdom (except that she is not very funny). In the house of Lady Wisdom, there is true contentment, the fulfilment of what a human being is created to be. 'Happy is the one who listens to me . . . whoever finds me finds life' (Proverbs 8.34–35).

Two invitations, two households, two destinies – this is the theme of the opening chapters of Proverbs. They speak of the drama that is constantly being acted out in the very seat and core of our personality, the essence of us that we call the 'soul'. The choices that face us in our early years might seem to define for ever the path we take: 'I took the one less traveled by, and that has made all the difference', as Robert Frost put it in his famous poem 'The Road Not Taken'. Perhaps the author of Proverbs is a sadder and a wiser man who knows only too well that adulthood continues to present us with choices we thought we had resolved years ago. The battle for the possession of the soul goes on all our lives, for choices confront us at every turn. If I am to serve God as best I can, what do I need to *do*? What do I really want to *be*? *Whose* do I want to be? To put it in the language of the Sermon on the Mount, where is my treasure, and therefore where is my heart? These questions will not go away. If anything, they are even more intense with age, as we become more aware of our endless capacity for deceiving ourselves.

The questions are the most fundamental a human being can ever face. The picture of the divided self is familiar from the seventh chapter of the letter to the Romans where Paul (surely the redeemed Paul who has found his faith in Christ) lays bare his spiritual distress: 'I do not do the good I want, but the evil I do not want is what I do . . . Wretched man that I am! Who will rescue me from this body of death?' (Romans 7.19, 24). It runs through the spiritual classics of every age: the *Confessions* of St Augustine, the *Divine Comedy* of Dante, John Bunyan's *The Pilgrim's Progress*, the poetry of John Donne and George Herbert, *The Interior Castle* of Teresa of Ávila, and the journals of Thomas Merton and Henri Nouwen. Most of these writers lived their Christianity in a very public way: a bishop, the head of a religious community, a dean, sought-after spiritual advisers. They knew better than anybody the risks religious leaders run. They never colluded with the temptation to be professional Christians.

Much of this book is concerned with the inner world of the minister, because it is from there that testimony and proclamation come. What goes on in the inner place of our human and Christian living is everything. At the centre of the Sermon on the Mount is the passage where Jesus teaches that the great works of religion – (in order) almsgiving, prayer and fasting – are to be practised 'in secret'. Why is this? Not that these works are in any sense *private*: far from it, for they belong to the public sphere of a community's life before God. But Jesus does insist that what is said and done *publicly* must originate in what is believed and practised *personally*: 'your Father who sees in secret will reward you' (Matthew 6.4, 6, 18). Lack integrity there, and we lack it everywhere. We end up with a false self that masks the truth, faking it like an actor playing a role, which is what the word 'hypocrite' (derived from the Greek *hypokritēs*) means.

How we attend to our own formation as ordained ministers, how we cultivate spiritual depth and insight, how we give ourselves to the calling and privilege of knowing God – these decisions are not very public or observable. We are not often asked whether we say our prayers or read the Bible, reflect on our experience or practise the presence of God in silence and meditation. And if we *are* asked to give an account of our spirituality, we easily acquire the art of fobbing the questioner off, and ourselves at the same time. But this is the antithesis of wisdom. Wisdom is to do what Jesus commands us: go into our room and shut the door, and be there as we would be with the world looking on. The philosopher Alfred North Whitehead defined religion as 'what a man does with his own solitude'. This is hardly an adequate definition of New Testament Christianity. Yet there is a truth in it that is verified, or falsified, every time we shut the door on our public role. In a lifetime of ministry, the evidence of how we are with ourselves in that private unobserved place eventually becomes manifest to everyone.

Oscar Wilde's novel *The Picture of Dorian Gray* is a dark parable that takes up this theme of what we are in secret. Taking its cue from the myths both of Faust and of Narcissus, it tells the story of a man obsessed with his own beauty to the extent that he will sell his own soul to preserve it. So the picture grows old while Gray keeps his youth, to the admiration of a *fin de siècle* society for whom external appearances are everything. But the portrait tells a more disturbing story than simply the natural ageing of a man. The lines on the face and the look of the eyes record a lifetime of decadence, self-indulgence and cruelty written into his features. The painting is too awful to display, so Gray hides it in a secret place. But he cannot resist visiting it every so often, and each time there is further evidence in the face of a cancerous corruption eating away at his life. Finally, in despair he slashes the portrait with a knife. When his friends come to the house to look for him, they find the body of an ugly, disfigured old man on the floor, cut to death with a knife; and on the wall, a portrait of a beautiful young man.

It is a powerful tale and a salutary one for those who have to live often in full view of others. We have seen how this relationship between the outer and inner worlds is played out in the stories of David and Solomon. There are, no doubt, a few clergy as corrupt as Dorian Gray, though I have never met any. But it would be a very unaware priest who did not take the lesson to heart and ponder what might be happening to his or her portrait hanging in secret, how it had changed over the years, and what the heavenly Father who sees in secret sees there.

To understand what is happening in secret and know what we are becoming, we need to visit our 'portrait' frequently. It's a commonplace of books on leadership and management that time on one's own is how values are properly embedded in personal life, because it is a place of truth. Equally, they stress that by itself, solitude is not enough. Time set aside with a skilled person for coaching and mentoring is regarded as indispensable for public effectiveness, for only then is a mirror held up to enable us to see ourselves as others see us.

The desert fathers of the early Christian centuries knew this. They sought solitude in the harsh, extreme conditions of the wilderness to heighten awareness of God and devote themselves to prayer. Monastic solitude was a school of discipleship: 'Go into your cell, and your cell will teach you everything.' Yet they knew the importance of being guided by others with insight and experience. 'Spiritual direction', as the Church knows it, has its origins in the relationships desert monks sought out with one another in order to nurture the life of the spirit. It draws on an even older tradition that we find in the wisdom writings, not least the early chapters of Proverbs, where personal guidance or instruction is an indispensable part of the formation of character. The relationship between solitude and spiritual direction is important. Psychoanalytic theories of childhood formation suggest the profound importance of playing in the company of the parent. Every parent knows how a child can be utterly absorbed in the activity of play, yet the presence of the father or mother is somehow not merely wanted but *needed*. It is a kind of solitude-in-company: 'being alone in the presence of another'. This is a creative way of understanding how insight and personal growth happen through psychotherapy. It allows the patient to 'play' by giving the freedom, in a safe space, to name and explore issues that it would be risky to open up anywhere else.

This way of safely 'holding' another person is familiar to clergy through their pastoral ministry, particularly at times of crisis. However, a welcome development of the last few decades has been the rediscovery of spiritual guidance as a long-term relationship in which to create space for spiritual growth. It has come to occupy a significant place in the work of many lay and ordained people. Some argue that the 'culture of narcissism' should not be reinforced by colluding with people's wish to talk endlessly about themselves. Yet all ministers know that there is no greater privilege than 'accompanying' another person on their journey as a human being and 'holding' that person in heart, mind and prayer. The tradition describes this as a special kind of friendship, a God-given relationship within the Church that is true Christian intimacy.

Its aim is truth-seeking, for friendship is always about truth. This search for truth can take the form of trying to 'map' the landscape of a life. It can be very practical in its focus on 'rule of life' issues such as prayer, Bible reading, eucharistic participation, study and retreat. Sacramental confession may be a regular part of it, as may be personal problem-solving or professional development. In all these ways the mirror of divine scrutiny is held up – for the tradition is clear that spiritual direction is not simply counselling or mentoring, but is an ecclesial relationship that exists to discern the will of God. And while this probably comes into the category of Archbishop Michael Ramsey's famous dictum 'All may, none must, some should' (his very Anglican way of speaking about the confessional), Hebrew wisdom and the desert fathers urge the importance of not imagining that we can make real spiritual progress without the help and guidance of others.

If this applies to all who are serious about their faith, it must apply especially to the ordained. I say this because of what they represent publicly. Our own spiritual growth is not something about which we can afford to be casual or indifferent – not, that is, if our own authenticity is at all important to us. For ministers to be 'alone in the presence of another' is in the spirit of those crucial central sections of the Sermon on the Mount we touched on earlier. If this has always been important, it is especially needed when the incidence of clergy stress, loss of confidence, marital break-up, exhaustion and burnout is worryingly high. In the matter of our own 'interior castle', it is at least as blessed to receive as it is to give. It is not simply the health of the clergy that is at stake here but the health of the Church of which they are themselves the spiritual leaders and guides. The Church's investment in the health of the clergy through the training of spiritual directors and the resourcing of other forms of support will be abundantly repaid.

How to live healthily, and how to make wise choices, is precisely the theme of Hebrew wisdom. The competing voices of Lady Wisdom and Dame Folly in the book of Proverbs are presented starkly as the choice between life and death. Every decision is potentially a decision for life or for death, even the apparently ordinary choices of daily living about which the maxims of the rest of the book of Proverbs have so much to say. The book seems to be saying that instruction into wisdom is to do with developing the habit of making life-giving decisions, while on the other hand, a thousand foolish decisions accumulate into a habit that erodes, diminishes and finally destroys life. For whereas Dame Folly's house turns out to be a dismal tumbrel that deposits her guests in Sheol, Lady Wisdom is none other than the speaker who can say of herself that 'the LORD created me at the beginning of his work . . . and I was daily his delight, rejoicing before him always' (Proverbs 8.22, 30). Formation in the way of wisdom is not simply about education for life (though it is that): it is a call to walk in the path that begins and ends in God. And even if we have wandered from it, the invitation is there, again and again. Lady Wisdom never stops calling and hoping.

Like Lady Wisdom, the Eucharist invites us to 'eat of my bread and drink of the wine I have mixed'. It is never too late to lay aside foolishness at the altar of God: whatever we have done, however prodigal we have been, Love bids us welcome. And Love can shine through even a very flawed life, as the memory of David shows. We sit and eat, and Wisdom entertains us; and we learn once more where health and happiness lie, and how, as those who are seeking wisdom, we can invite others to walk with us towards them.

7

An ordered life:
Psalm 1

———⟡———

There is a French word beloved of all wine-bibbers: *terroir*.
There is no real English equivalent to it. It means the environment of a vineyard that gives it its unique character. It is an
alchemy of the soil and its underlying geology, its altitude and
microclimate, the direction it faces, how well watered it is,
whether it is on a hillside or in a valley, the history of the
terrain and how the soil has been worked down the centuries,
even how near it is to a main road. The wines of the Chablis
Grand Cru, for instance, owe their greatness (and their price)
largely to the fact that the vines are grown in a bowl in the
hills on a tiny area of soil with a rare geology known as Kim-
meridgian: these are the defining ingredients of their *terroir*.
Move a score of metres off that geology, and the wines are
mere *vin de table* without an *appellation* between them. One
degree of latitude reverses the whole of viticulture. To make
good wine, it is not enough to be proficient in the mechanical
crafts of wine making or understand the chemistry of fer-
mentation: you have to know about geology, meteorology,
botany, social geography and cultural history. You need to
know the *terroir*.

Psalm 1 is about the *terroir* of the wise man or woman
whose life is set on God, and whose delight is in YHWH's
instruction or *torah*, what we familiarly know in the English
versions as the law of the Lord. This life-giving environment
is like the prosperous *terroir* belonging to the tree planted by

84

streams of water which yields its fruit and whose leaves do not wither. Its stable, rooted abundance is in absolute contrast to the evanescence of the dry chaff blown away across the waterless landscape, which is how the psalm likens the career of the unrighteous, what Ecclesiastes calls *hebel*, vanity, nothingness. It's the familiar image of the two ways of righteousness and wickedness that we met in the previous chapter, where they were personified as Lady Wisdom and Dame Folly.

The book of Psalms is principally a collection of songs (literally, 'praises') that had their origin in the worship of Israel's temple and sanctuaries. They belonged to the public world of ceremonial and liturgy. (This is true even of most of the psalms written in the first-person singular, the 'I' psalms. We should imagine the individual bringing his or her experience of suffering or thanksgiving into the temple so that it could be 'offered' to God through the medium of liturgical worship and music.) But the time came when the Israelites no longer had a temple or even a land to call their own. In exile, the community turned to more personal and intimate ways of prayer and worship. This kind of piety was centred on prayer and the study of the scriptures, both in small assemblies (the origin of the synagogue) and alone. Many Jews did not return to their ancestral land when the official exile came to an end, the Jerusalem temple was rebuilt and liturgical worship restored. They remained scattered across the ancient world in *diaspora*. In a pagan world, this might well have put their identity at risk. However, the opposite proved true. Diaspora Judaism flourished and became enormously influential in the development of the Jewish faith. The scriptures, over time formally identified as authorized books belonging to a 'canon' or 'rule', became the badge of Jewish identity. This was particularly true of the core texts of the *torah*, the 'books of Moses' which told the stories of Israel's origins as YHWH's own people, and set out their obligations to him through the covenant.

Psalm 1 breathes this atmosphere of meditative personal piety. It introduces the book of Psalms by setting them in the context of 'the law of the Lord'. It's no accident that the Psalter is divided into five books, an echo of the five books of the *torah*, Genesis to Deuteronomy. It's as if the compilers of the Psalter wanted to promote it as a poetic commentary on the teaching of the law. The study of *torah* 'day and night', says the psalm, is the only safe guide to living as God intends. So it invites the reader to enter into the psalms as illustrating the way of life spelled out in the *torah*. If (suggests the psalm) we want to know how to be faithful to God's covenant through thick and thin, read the psalms. For they open a window on to the souls of believers down the ages. Through the lived experience of worshippers whether collectively or personally, in lament and celebration, the psalms give instruction in walking God's way of righteous wisdom. They model what it means to be loyal to the law of the Lord.

We have seen how wisdom in Israel is about living a well-ordered life. Order is the character of the created world, and wisdom teaches men and women to emulate it in themselves. This is a constant theme in Proverbs; for instance, famously, its advice to the lazy or indolent: 'Go to the ant, you lazybones; consider its ways and be wise. Without having any chief or officer or ruler, it prepares its food in summer, and gathers its sustenance in harvest' (Proverbs 6.6–8). Disorder by contrast is a threat to the very fabric of existence. It is its negation, its denial, like the mythological monsters of the chaotic deep whom the gods had to subdue and put in their place if life was to be sustained. And our psalm, in drawing the sharp contrast between a life that has a shape defined by *torah* and an existence (you can't call it a life) that has no direction or purpose, sets out what we could call a human and spiritual *terroir* for the formation of the man or woman of God. If we want to discover the kind of environment in which we will flourish in the service of God, the wisdom tradition will guide us.

What is the *terroir*, the spiritual environment and context, in which ministers will flourish?

Let me mention once more the place where my ministry is currently mainly exercised. For half its life, Durham Cathedral was a Benedictine cathedral priory and lived according to the Rule of St Benedict. At the heart of the Rule lies a vision of life that is balanced, ordered and stable. The fountainhead of all the activity of the monastery was the praise of God, the seven-times-a-day and once-a-night round of prayer and worship that Benedict called 'the work of God'. Attached to the church is the cloister that linked prayer with the rest of life: the dormitory, the refectory, the kitchen, the scriptorium, library, chapter house and parlour or slype. These spaces all testify to the multifarious activity of a large monastery. There was daily work to do to maintain the life of the convent and transact its business. There was the requirement on the monks to study the scriptures and other writings. There was the singing of psalms to rehearse, and manuscripts to copy out. There were estates to be managed, novices to educate, guests to be welcomed and the sick and poor to be cared for. There were the ordinary human needs of the monks to be met: eating and drinking, sleeping, washing, conversing at times allowed by the Rule.

We can read the *terroir* of a Benedictine community from the way the architecture is laid out. What the architecture tells us is how all these tasks were seen as the offering of life in its totality, the summation of spiritual, intellectual, manual and human effort in a common life given to God. The vow of stability is a commitment to a particular place for life, but it is also an image of the human person remade and rebuilt on the secure foundation that is Christ. This, for Benedict, is the goal: not the well ordering of the monastery for its own sake, but because this is a place where disciples are formed. He says, at the conclusion:

We have established a school for the Lord's service, and hope to order nothing that is harsh or rigorous. But if anything be somewhat strictly laid down, for the amendment of vices or the preservation of charity, do not therefore fly in dismay from the path of salvation, whose beginning cannot but be strait and difficult. But as we go forward in our life and in faith, we shall with hearts enlarged and unspeakable sweetness of love run the way of God's commandments; so that never departing from his guidance but persevering in his teaching in the monastery until death, we may by patience share in the sufferings of Christ, that we may deserve to be partakers of his kingdom.

It would be tempting here to embark on another book called 'St Benedict for Ministers'. I must be content to make a few connections that may prompt further thought. The first of these is to draw attention to the fundamental point about the Rule that emerges clearly from those words of conclusion. Benedict says, in effect, that before someone can be a good monk, he must first be a faithful disciple. To be a monk and make a commitment to the life of the monastery, is first to be a Christian and to be dedicated to a lifetime of following Jesus. We could say that those who undertake to live as 'exemplary Christians', that is, men or women taking on themselves the profession of a religious, and living out in front of others the monastic expression of Christianity, must first be sure that they are securely rooted in the gospel. To be a committed Christian is a necessary condition of living the monastic life.

It may sound obvious beyond words to translate this to the ordained ministry, but I believe that precisely the same is true of those who undertake to represent the Church publicly through ordination. They, too, are 'exemplary Christians' who are looked to not only by others in the Church but by the general public as those who are *ex animo* committed to living according to their own profession. We explored the 'public' and 'personal' aspects of ministry earlier in connection with the career of David, where serious dissonance between the two leads inevitably to public as well as private disarray. We may not like to think of ourselves as 'exemplary Christians'; we may deny that we are in any sense 'special', and we would be right to do so. Yet what ministers *model* is undeniably as important as what they *proclaim*. In an inchoate way, some start out on the journey towards ordination by recognizing in themselves a desire to be better disciples. Ordination can be seen as a way of becoming 'closer to Jesus'. They soon learn, of course, that being a religious professional, with its daily proximity to word and sacraments, does not of itself make anyone more holy; and yet it can't be wrong to question the motive altogether. If we do not demonstrate seriousness in the way we practise our own Christianity, who is going to pay attention to our public ministry?

Benedict can help us in this. He is saying that Christian seriousness means creating a *terroir* in which discipleship can be nurtured. For most of us, this *terroir* is not a monastery in which a total community lives in physical spaces each of which is assigned a specific purpose and meaning. Yet the ideal can be translated into an attitude to ministry that helpfully draws on the insight that shape, rhythm, pattern and structure are necessary to the good ordering of life, with time allocated in realistic ways to its primary tasks. This isn't to deny the 'secular' nature of ordained ministry in most churches today, whose clergy are not living or pretending to live under a monastic rule. It is to suggest that some kind of simple rules of life, worked out in the light of personal circumstances and regularly reviewed as they change, is helpful and even necessary. Whether or not it is written down, the aim of a rule is to try to express how the minister lives before God. This is as much an exercise in healthy self-awareness and truth-seeking as it is of aspiration and resolve. (To be realistic, I doubt if any of us can get very far with this difficult exercise in honest self-scrutiny without the help of a spiritual director or guide, through whose wisdom and friendship we learn to see ourselves without illusion or fantasy.)

What shape might such a rule take? I suggest a quadrilateral of four fundamental aspects.

First, *prayer*. This is what the monastery was *for*. At a more profound level, this is what all human beings are *for*: the praise and worship of God. For Benedict, the divine office was the *opus Dei*, the work of God. One sense of those words is to take them as meaning the 'work' we do for God in offering our worship as creatures to their Creator. Yet the phrase also means God's work in us, recognizing that what we offer to God is what he himself has first given us. It recalls us to the dynamic of grace and response, God's movement towards creation in generosity and goodness, reciprocated by our movement back to him in wonder, love and praise. The *opus Dei* is the celebration of God's creative and redemptive love articulated on our own behalf, but also on behalf of creation. It means the offering of the whole of life in worship, lament as well as thanksgiving, its personal as well as its public dimensions. It is both what we do together in *common prayer* (such as the reciting of the daily office) and what we do as individuals as we grow in our love of God: times for personal prayer, silence and meditation, retreat, spiritual direction – all aspects of *habitus* that make for spiritual health and wellbeing.

Second, *study*. Benedict uses the word *lectio* to encompass the various kinds of reading a monk was obliged to do (and it's worth reminding ourselves that in the Middle Ages when the vast majority of the populace could not read, monasteries with their libraries were highly exceptional as centres of learning and literacy). By far the most important aspect of *lectio* was the study of the Bible. Perhaps we shouldn't take for granted that all today's ministers not only study the scriptures but *love* them, though it ought to be inconceivable that the preparation of the Sunday sermon should not involve studying, as well as applying, the texts given for the day. But if I am right to take from the story of Joseph the insight that the minister is an interpreter and theologian in the world, then 'study' is simply a *sine qua non* if he or she is to give an intelligent account of the Church's faith in a sceptical world. This means not only what we call 'theology' in the strict sense, but the maintaining of a good 'hinterland' through (for example) novels, biography, politics, science, the arts, news media – all these could be key aspects of learning to 'read' the world in which we live and minister. The possibilities for acquiring a well-stocked mind, so prized by the wisdom writers, are endless.

Third, *work*. If prayer and study are both 'work', this suggests that all of life is 'work' in the sense that the ultimate task of being alive is the 'work' of becoming a fully human being. As part of this, physical work (as distinct from spiritual or intellectual work) has an honoured place in Benedict's Rule, again a reflection of the dignity given to it in the wisdom tradition. The physical work of ordained ministry is not always easy to define, still less condense to a heading in a rule of life. It is a wonderful cluster of activities through which ministry serves the Church and the world. It includes pastoral care, education, evangelism, hospitality, spiritual guidance, social justice, and the governance and management of the Church. What elevates these tasks from merely being 'jobs' and gives them a humane and a spiritual quality is their relationship to prayer and study; that is, how they are informed by the way we pray and the way we understand how God is at work in the world. This is to dignify the work of ministry with a truly theological (and therefore ultimate) value. It is done 'for God' as well as for others or ourselves. It has its own validity, and this is what a rule of life aims to capture.

Fourth, *recreation*. Benedict does not have a word for 'leisure'; indeed, it's doubtful that anyone in pre-modern times other than the very affluent would have understood the concept or have had the time to think about it. However, the more evocative word 'recreation' does echo Benedict's vision of a community that is genuinely 'creative', and therefore daily imitating the life-giving creativity of God. Today in the West, leisure is an industry that pervades every aspect of life, including decisions about how time and money are spent on it. In their attitude to leisure, clergy have an opportunity to model something extremely important. We should see this not as 'time off' so much as sabbatical time for rest, renewal, the deepening of our personal relationships, the cultivation of our own humanity, and the opportunity to enjoy the good earth God has placed us in. The capacity to be kind to oneself is a mark of wisdom. In the output-driven, activity-focused world of the Church today, this is an issue with which many clergy grapple, sometimes paying a high price in mental or physical health. To live by a rule with a healthy balance between work and leisure could be life-saving.

This speaks powerfully in a world of shifting values and an uncertain future. This was exactly the world St Benedict knew, with the collapse of the Roman Empire and the order it had established in Europe. How do we who have our hope set on Christ achieve some measure of stability? This vision of the wisely ordered life lived according to a principle or rule in which recreation, work, study and prayer are in harmony with one another is deeply attractive. Its potential significance in public ministry, both in giving it shape and integrity, and for what it models about being Christian in the world, is clear enough. Most clergy know from their own experience how easily the pressures and crises of ordained life, not to mention the temptations of money, sex and power, tend to subvert it. In the imagery of the psalm, they pollute the *terroir* and erode the soil in which we are being grown, so that our roots gradually loosen their hold and (to return to the psalm), we are like the chaff, at the mercy of the first wind that blows. This is how we have read the career of Solomon who started out so well and whose reign ended with the kingdom on the brink of collapse. To those on the threshold of ministry, it is inconceivable that their longings might ever be other than noble when all thoughts and ambitions are wholeheartedly to love and serve God and the world. Yet time reveals how real the personal risks of public ministry are. Wisdom says: these need to be realistically understood, and a way of life arrived at that is sustainable.

What is this all *for*? The answer is, in the words of a commonly used phrase, so that we can become 'reflective practitioners'. This means doing the 'work' of ministry with what wisdom in the Bible calls 'insight', alive to its meaning and purpose in God's scheme of things. It means being as alert to the *why* of ordained ministry as to the *how*. 'Their delight is in the law of the LORD, and on his law they meditate day and night,' says Psalm 1 in a sentiment echoed in other wisdom psalms such as 19 and 119. This is the clue to creating the healthy environment that will 'grow' a human being to the measure of the stature of the fullness of Christ. It's the God-given *terroir* for every minister who cares not simply about professional development but about all that goes into making a man or woman complete in Jesus Christ. The psalm says that this is the way that life becomes fruitful and fulfilled, rather than empty and devoid of meaning. In a world in which so many do not even recognize their desires and hungers for what they truly are, the *terroir* that shapes what we model is worth a lifetime's investment.

8

Envy, worship and understanding:
Psalm 73

—————»•«—————

What is the besetting sin of Western civilization in the twenty-first century?

A trawl through the seven deadly sins suggests a number of plausible candidates. Greed, pride, wrath, lust are old-fashioned words that sit uneasily in the vocabulary of modernity. Yet they draw attention to where our true values lie. The best indicator of the values we live by is to examine our priorities and desires. What we think we want or need is closely related to what we think we *are* and how we think we should live.

Although pride is classically regarded by moral theologians as the worst of the deadly sins, it may not necessarily be the most pervasive, at least in our own society. There is another, more insidious, candidate. The famous twentieth-century psychoanalyst Melanie Klein wrote a highly influential paper on how children grow up to become mature adults, and what gets in the way of the healthy development of the human psyche. It was called *Envy and Gratitude*. She argues that the besetting problem of humanity that underlies all our conflicts and struggles and alienation is envy. We learn it (literally) at our mother's breast, for the root of envy is the primordial fear that what we have and need might be taken away from us and given to someone else; for if nothing is left to us, then we die. Envy, she says, is what drives our need to possess, to dominate, to succeed. There is only one way to break this spiral of destructiveness and despair: what she called *Dankbarheit*, gratitude that what we have is enough to sustain our lives and bring us to achieve our potential as men and women. To transfer another epithet from the literature of psychoanalysis, it is 'good enough' for what we need.

In the wisdom literature, envy is regarded as at least as destructive as pride. Two of the wisdom psalms focus on it in ways that show acute insight into how it poisons even the best attitudes and motives. Psalm 37 is an A to Z on the subject of envy – literally, for the psalm plays on the 22 letters of the Hebrew alphabet from *aleph* to *tau* as if to say, here is a child's way of learning the hardest of life's lessons, 'do not be envious of wrongdoers' but 'trust in the Lord and do good'. It is perhaps easier to state than to do. Many is the worshipper who has wondered, when the psalm is sung in cathedrals on the seventh evening of every month, whether life is always as simple as the ageing psalmist makes out. Even as a young student I used to be haunted by the famous (some would say notorious) verse from this psalm inscribed in Latin above the high table of my college dining hall: 'I have been young, and now am old: and yet saw I never the righteous forsaken, nor his seed begging their bread' (Psalm 37.25, BCP). Is this the too-easy speech of a privileged writer who had never come across the people the Old Testament describes as God's poor?

More searching and more passionate is the exploration of envy in Psalm 73. Here the psalmist vividly describes his own experience of those he calls the 'arrogant'. Their lives are without pain or trouble. They get away with all manner of corruption and exploitation. They enjoy wealth and prosperity, and as if that were not enough, they are celebrities as well: 'Therefore the people turn and praise them, and find no fault in them' (v. 10). The effect on the psalmist is to wonder why he ever bothered with religion. 'All in vain I have kept my heart clean and washed my hands in innocence. For all day long I have been plagued, and am punished every morning'

95

(vv. 13–14). The practice of faith is more trouble than it's worth. It imposes constraints we might prefer to live without. It denies us opportunities for self-advancement and pleasure. It doesn't make us rich or successful, or even especially contented – this is the psalmist's experience.

This analysis of the human condition is familiar to anyone who takes faith seriously. In particular, I think it is recognizable to many clergy, especially those in middle age and beyond who see life slipping away from them without having realized the success and prosperity enjoyed by many of their school or college contemporaries. In my work as a spiritual adviser, I have listened to priests who, while not regretting sacrificing other possible careers for the sake of being ordained, nevertheless find it hard not to envy the salaries and houses of their peers. It isn't that a priest's stipend is impossible to live on. It's more that in an acquisitive society where consumerism is all, envy is an almost unstoppable emotion. When the object of envy is the success of the many people who care little for God and nothing for the Church, self-doubt in vocation and even in faith is both a natural and an understandable response. The cynical slogan of the arrogant, 'How can God know? Is there knowledge in the Most High?' (verse 11) is easy to echo as the cry of resignation from an envious and disconsolate heart. Practical atheism is disconcertingly contagious.

How this is turned round in the psalm is striking. It happens through one of those shafts of illumination that enable us to see a situation in an entirely new way. 'When I thought how to understand this, it seemed to me a wearisome task, until I went into the sanctuary of God' (vv. 16–17). The place of worship provides a different perspective, a renewed vision of life and its dilemmas. There is only so much that agonized wrestling with the inner demons of envy can do, and for the psalmist it is 'wearisome'. This is because he recognizes that envy is fundamentally a spiritual issue that has to be approached in a religious way. This calls for a stance that only faith can give. This is what the 'sanctuary' symbolizes.

But the sanctuary is more than a metaphor of faith: it's a place where a specific activity takes place, namely the worship of God. So the psalmist is saying that it is through the activity of worship that envy is addressed and attitudes fundamentally changed. Worship proves to be a redemptive and transformative experience. It gives him access, so to speak, to God's way of seeing things. He views life's ups and downs *sub specie aeternitatis*, and from here the fortunes of the arrogant look rather different. As a worshipper, he sees how their 'end' (as both purpose and destiny) is slippery and unstable. In contrast to the unreality of life governed by material success, the psalmist now knows where true and lasting joy belongs. 'Whom have I in heaven but you? And there is nothing on earth that I desire other than you. My flesh and my heart may fail, but God is the strength of my heart and my portion for ever' (vv. 25–26). He has travelled a long way since the psalm's opening verses. Then, he believed that 'God is good to the upright' as no more than a formal religious affirmation. Now he knows it in his heart.

Wisdom writing tends to be reticent about worship. The 'cult', by which we mean the public worship of temple and sanctuary, does not loom large in any of the texts we are exploring. Wisdom tends to adopt an understated attitude to 'organized religion' that contrasts with other parts of the Old Testament where cultic practice is a major concern. There, how worship is offered, how its ceremonial is governed, how the temple is understood in the life of the community, and most importantly of all, how all this relates to the moral and ethical basis of Israel's life, are major concerns. We can speculate as to why the wise seem not to have been unduly preoccupied by these matters. But given this reticence, it's all the more striking that a wisdom writer should place his transformed understanding of the world in the sanctuary. It's as if, in his tradition, there is a presumption that difficulties and dilemmas should be susceptible to a rational explanation. The fact is, they are not. Only as he 'goes to church' and worships his Creator is this vital disclosure given, when it all becomes clear.

This is a critically important insight for those serving in the Church's ministry. If you ask the public what they think the job of the clergy is, most people would answer that it's to take services, preach sermons and say prayers. They would not be wrong: leading, preparing and managing worship is the most visible aspect of ministry where what we believe and practise as the Church and its clergy is very much on public display. Yet many congregations have ceased to have very high expectations of churchgoing. People go to church for many reasons, but anticipating (or even wanting) a life-changing encounter with the living God is not necessarily one of them. They do not expect to go out of church touched and changed in some way by the liturgy or the sermon. And over the years, a congregation's lack of expectation or even its palpable sense of boredom begin to erode the minister's own belief in the importance of what he or she is doing as a liturgical leader and president. From being the apex of the work of ministry in which all of life is offered and celebrated, the liturgy can become just another routine.

Yet the psalm invites us to think again about the part the 'sanctuary' plays in human life. It suggests that one of the effects of public worship ought to be *reorientation*. I mean by this both a new awareness of life as God intends it to be, and the consequence of this way of seeing things, which is the realignment of attitude, motive and desire towards the love of God. For the psalmist, this led to his seeing his envy for what it was and the recovery of what alone was worth coveting, the presence of God himself. For the prophet Isaiah attending temple worship, his vision of God's unutterable holiness resulted in his understanding for the first time his own complicity in the corruption of his own people, and from this sprang his vocation to be a prophet to them (Isaiah 6). St Paul says that when we eat the bread and share the cup of Communion, we 'proclaim the Lord's death until he comes' (1 Corinthians 11.26). The Greek word here has a strong missionary connotation. It means that the liturgy is always an announcement of the gospel. John Wesley says that the sacrament is a 'converting ordinance'. To celebrate the Eucharist is to be mission-shaped.

I am saying, then, that to preside at the liturgy is to be a leader in mission. This is not always understood or appreciated, either by congregations in local churches or by clergy themselves. Very often, liturgy is seen to be one kind of activity, and mission another. And pressed to extremes, liturgy becomes a 'bad' word because it is 'churchy', and therefore presumed to be an essentially private activity unrelated to the world and its needs; while mission is a 'good' word that expresses attempts at relevance through outreach and social concern. This split is not only not helpful, it is deeply unbiblical and untheological. It subverts the integrity of the Church's vocation in two ways. It robs the liturgy of its proper embrace of God's world by which life is sanctified and offered with all the profound life-changing consequences that follow. It also robs the Church's outreach of its roots in corporate prayer and worship, without which its witness to the kingdom of God collapses into a merely human enterprise. (On this point, if we ever find ourselves speaking of 'building' or 'extending' the kingdom, we should examine our assumptions carefully: the kingdom of God is not some social or evangelistic programme we undertake, but a divine event that we welcome with joy and testify to.)

As a young parish priest in a market town in the north of

England, I needed to learn the importance of this. In particular, my role as celebrant extended well beyond the boundaries of the regular Sunday congregation. Far from merely being a chaplain to that gathered community, I began to see how the Church's worship 'represents' and makes conscious the unarticulated worship of creation. That insight about the priestly role of the Church can be over-used as a comforting way of theologizing to ourselves on the enduring significance of what we do as churchgoing declines, though its importance lies in both affirming the presence of God in the world and bringing within the ambit of his love human suffering and pain. But in day-to-day ministry, the role of liturgical president seemed increasingly to become a key focus of my ministry. There were special services for the town and its many institutions, such as civic services for mayor-making, fair time and Remembrance. There was a large number of the occasional offices, baptisms, weddings and funerals that are the staple of every parish incumbent. And of course there was the Sunday service, which was billed, importantly, not as a 'Family Communion' but as the 'Parish' Eucharist, an act of worship that tried to celebrate and offer the life of a whole human community.

One little fact of parish life struck me as significant at the time, and I have often pondered it since. In this traditional Church of England set-up, there were the offices of Morning and Evening Prayer which, as canon law still requires, were celebrated each day in the parish church. Next to the churchyard was a retirement home. Elderly ladies sat for long hours at their windows and would note every coming and going along the path to the church porch. It was instantly noticed when, as occasionally happened (for good reason, I need to add) the clergy were not to be seen making their way twice daily across the churchyard, and the bell did not toll. Within hours it was noised around the town that the vicar had missed his prayers that day. No doubt some of this is just the small-town interest of people with time on their hands, and I did not read too much into that – all clergy get used to living in the world of a Barbara Pym novel. But once, in the shops, someone I barely knew asked me if anything had been wrong the previous day because I had not been into the church, and people knew (as they knew most things) that it was not my regular free day. 'You weren't at your prayers,' said this person, and then I understood what this was really all about. It was not simply that I had not been at public prayer for *them*, i.e. for the parish, nor that I had not been attending to my own spiritual health. It was that I had not *done my duty* as a parish priest, which was taken to mean presiding at worship day by day in the house of God.

In these ways, I saw how my role as a priest was to interpret the life of both community and individuals in the light of faith in God. This is one of the prime functions of the liturgy. It happens as we allow ceremony, preaching and the pastoral care that surrounds them to answer the question: what is God saying and doing in this service? How does this celebration, this lament, this rite of passage, this Sunday Eucharist, this daily act of prayer make connections between God's story and our own? How does it help us to see what life would be like if God were in charge of the world, the parish, or my own personal existence? What does God affirm of our lives at this point in their history, and what does he challenge? Or to put it in the language of Psalm 73, what *meaning* lies in what we do before God in the sanctuary, and how does it change us?

In this book I have already said something about wisdom as the search for meaning, and how one of the roles of a minister is to be an interpreter. It's clear from the wisdom literature that 'insight' is the gift of a wise God to those who search for it. It's also clear that it needs to be 'grown' in us: the tragedy of Solomon is that he did not nurture the remarkable gifts he had been given at the outset of his reign. And the nurture of wisdom is more than cultivating a reflective approach to life. The psalm suggests that the interpretation of meanings comes in a public as well as a private place. The 'sanctuary of God' is both *God's* space set apart for divine purposes, but also the *community's* space where its business with God is transacted. In the encounter with God that is worship, the sanctuary is charged with new perspectives on human life. We see what we could become, what the world could become. We see how the kingdom of God utterly transforms our 'take' on things. We see a new heaven and a new earth as if this world were already gathered up in the crucifixion and resurrection of Jesus Christ.

In his book *On Liturgical Theology*, Aidan Kavanagh makes the striking point that the primary theologians of the Church are Mrs Murphy and her parish priest at worship. Their

> discourse in faith is carried on not by concepts and propositions nearly so much as in the vastly complex vocabulary of experiences had, prayers said, sights seen, smells smelled, words said and heard and responded to, emotions controlled and released, sins committed and repented, children born and loved ones buried, and in many other ways no one can count or always account for.
> (Minnesota: Liturgical Press, 1992, p. 147)

He means that as we celebrate the Eucharist, we are given a language in which to speak about God and his purposes; we enter most profoundly into the vision of a world redeemed by the grace and mercy of God in Jesus; and we participate in that life-giving transformation for ourselves.

Mrs Murphy is an implicit theologian, for she knows and loves God, but she lacks the discourse to enable her to make this explicit. Her priest has the discourse, but the theory is not enough to make him a theologian either. They need each other, and they both need the 'sanctuary', with its liturgy and its community, in order to be true theologians – or, as I am putting it, to become wise. 'It is not just something she and her pastor think or say, but something they taste, the air they breathe.' It is where they understand, at the profoundest level, 'what it really means when God pours himself out into humanity, into the world as a member of our race. Nowhere else can that primary body of perceived data be read so well as in the living tradition of Christian worship.'

How do we set about creating life-changing liturgy that makes people wise in this way?

It would take a different book to begin to answer that question, which is as much about the *arts* and *crafts* of worship as its theology. But all the arts and crafts in the world will not be enough without conviction at the core of liturgy as to *why* it matters so much. If humanity exists to glorify its Creator and to make conscious the worship of creation, then worship is the most fundamental activity we can ever engage in. We are never more human than when we are at prayer and taste something of the life of God himself. For the psalmist, embittered and diminished by his envy, the 'sanctuary' became the place of proper perspective and the enlargement of his soul. There he glimpsed God and knew what he really wanted and needed in life. That is the answer to the question, often asked in cathedrals especially, *why* so much effort and resource is put into the worship of God. If what we are about in the 'sanctuary' is nothing less than transformation, then it is right that it should cost a good deal, perhaps even, in T. S. Eliot's famous words, 'not less than everything'.

This is a far cry from the Sunday morning entertainments that pass for worship in some unfortunate churches, and from the dead hand of liturgical routine (which is worse) that infects others. To see the minister as a master of ceremonies (or its feminine equivalent) is not to demean the role into some kind of obsessive cult functionary whose only bedtime reading is *Ritual Notes*. Far from it. If we can begin to see how liturgy opens doors of perception and opportunity, then its preparation and offering is ultimately the profoundest commitment we can make both to mission and to the pastoral and spiritual formation of the worshipping community. To be the parish liturgist is not different from being the parish theologian, pastor, prophet and missioner. For all these roles are about God's purpose to change lives, restore the fallen, heal the broken and make all things new.

When the psalmist left the sanctuary with his reorientated vision, it was with a testimony to share with the world. 'For me it is good to be near God; I have made the Lord GOD my refuge, to tell of all your works' (Psalm 73.28). That sums up the aim of all ministry, which is to bring other people to the point where they make that testimony their own, in the hope, the prayer and the fervent expectation that one day it will become the new song of all creation.

9

Witness to suffering:
Job

—————

I experienced the desert, once, for about an hour. It was at
Masada, that huge rock that rises 800 feet sheer above the
western shore of the Dead Sea. Herod the Great had a fort-
ress there, and then the Romans. In AD 66 it was seized by
Jewish insurgents who held it for more than four years in a
last defiant stand against the empire. After a long siege the
Romans finally breached it, whereupon its 960 occupants, apart
from seven women and children, killed themselves in a
suicide pact. They destroyed all their possessions except their
stockpiles of food, so that the Romans would know they had
not starved the Jews into submission.

I was there on a pilgrimage. We had travelled down from
Jerusalem to Jericho, past Qumran where the Dead Sea Scrolls
were discovered, and the beautiful oasis of En Gedi. There are
cable cars to whisk you to the top of Masada in a few minutes.
But my mind was full of the visit I had made to the Holocaust
Memorial in Jerusalem, Yad Vashem, the day before. I wanted
to *do* something to honour my Jewish forebears who had perished here all those centuries ago, make some small gesture at
this extraordinary place.

So a friend and I set out to walk to the top. Our Israeli guide
said we must be deranged to go out into the midday sun, and
declared that he took no responsibility for our safety. He might
have added that even Josephus says you take your life in your
hands on this rock. We could see the steep path called the 'snake'

winding upwards. We thought: 800 feet, not even half the height of Kinder Scout; there are benches with canopies on the way up; we have a litre of water each, sun hats, creams . . . A hundred yards along, we realized what we had taken on. The sun beat down out of a sky like brass. The heat seemed to press us into the unforgiving rocks. There was not the flicker of a breeze. Our colleagues waved cheerily from the cable car that glided improbably above us. All around us was aridity: nothing lived here. We walked at some distance from each other: this was not a place in which to talk. I thought of little else but water, shelter and rest. We had to stop frequently. So this was the desert: terrible in its beauty, godforsaken, liable to drive you mad. Severed from the umbilical cords of bus and cable car, we felt not a little fearful. We staggered to the top, and there was wood and concrete to walk on, ice-creams and souvenirs on sale where 1,000 people had died. A man collected tickets: a moment of true bathos. When it was time to go down, we took the cable car and headed in our buses for the spa, a salty swim in the Dead Sea, and cool drinks and salads in an air-conditioned restaurant.

For an hour, we had ceased to be tourists and began to *participate* in the desert, experience its grasp on us, its demand. For an hour we had taken a tentative step into this harsh, disorientating wilderness – an hour's isolation from the reassuring comforts of civilization. An hour does not give God much time. Yet I did glimpse, I believe, how the desert is a place of truth or reorientation that strips the spirit bare of pretence and illusion. I began to glimpse the importance of this place of living death for Israel's long years of journeying towards their own land, and for Jesus at the outset of his ministry. It is as if suffering is deeply embedded into the story of both Testaments from their very inception. And this is to reflect how it is one of the universal themes of humanity. None of us is a stranger to suffering, even if not all of us experience it to the same extent. Pain is part of the human condition.

In the book of Job, Hebrew wisdom recognizes the central place suffering has in the story all human beings tell. Job is called 'a blameless and upright man who fears God and turns away from evil'. In the prose prologue to the book (chapters 1 and 2), he is precisely the kind of man envisaged by Psalm 37, which as we saw in the last chapter is an A to Z about how the wise sufferer faces evil. He is stable, contemplative, serene, not given to anger, anxiety or fretfulness, endowed with spiritual equanimity and the far-sightedness that takes the long view, in all things trusting in the Lord and waiting patiently for him. 'You have heard of the patience of Job.' The poetic speeches present a rather different picture, however. There, in the drama acted out among the ashes, an altogether more passionate man lays bare his internal conflicts and faces his demons, arguing with God, arguing with his friends, arguing with himself and cursing the day of his birth. This too is wisdom, for the book of Job is rightly regarded as the greatest of all the wisdom writings for the depth of its insights into the human condition, and for the unflinching way it brings religious faith face to face with the reality of suffering.

One of the aspects of Solomon's wisdom we have noticed in the story about him is his knowledge of the natural world. 'He would speak of trees, from the cedar that is in the Lebanon to the hyssop that grows in the wall; he would speak of animals, and birds, and reptiles, and fish' (1 Kings 4.33). This is of a piece with other wisdom books, which abound in references to nature as examples of an ordered world that teaches human beings how to live, if only they have eyes to see. At first sight, that patterned, well-shaped world seems very different from the turbulent, chaotic journey through suffering that is charted in the book of Job.

But these are of course simply different aspects of the same reality. To explore and celebrate the natural world and to recognize its physical order is at once to be confronted by questions about 'order' in a deeper sense: why does the universe appear not to exhibit a *moral* and *spiritual* order as well? Why do the wicked prosper and the righteous suffer? Why are not both rewarded fairly for their deeds? And why, especially, is there undeserved pain in the world? What meaning attaches to a universe that doesn't play by the rules, and what value therefore can a puny individual's life possibly carry? These are among the profoundest and most difficult questions of human existence. Among the evidence that biblical wisdom is genuinely 'wise' is that it faces these questions squarely: in psalms such as 37 and 73, in Ecclesiastes and most famously of all, in the book of Job. And because ministry in the Church is inevitably concerned with these things, it's appropriate that they should occupy us towards the end of this book.

This is not the place to discuss theodicy, the study of how to vindicate the goodness and justice of God in the face of suffering. Ministers are, it is true, expected to speak authoritatively about theodicy, though it is seldom appropriate in a pastoral situation, and there are few who can do it convincingly. Yet the problem of suffering, like the poor, is always with us. Good theology can never sidestep it, nor content itself with easy answers. Poverty and pain will always need to be the special concern of the ordained, because they *care* both about those who suffer and about where God is to be found in relation to it. Like Joseph whom we saw earlier on in the role of interpreter, the minister is an interpreter of what is going on in the stories of human beings and in the world's story. He or she is learning to read experience in the light of faith in God's purposes and to invite faith-based reflection on it. This is what it is to be a theologian. If ordained ministry is to be a genuinely wise and *theological* activity and not just another caring profession, it will place suffering at the centre of its concerns. It has never been possible to speak publicly for the gospel and lead the prayer of the Church without doing this. But today's world makes this an especially sharp issue. In a media-driven environment, we are instantly made aware of the latest tragedies and disasters being played out across the planet. Any ministry that does not show a deeply felt awareness of and compassion for suffering, or that evades a thoughtful, intelligent response to it, is certainly inauthentic. The praise of God and the pain of the world belong together.

It is important to understand what the book of Job is about – and *not* about. Many have turned to it looking for answers to the problem of suffering. But this turns out not to be its purpose (or if it is, it signally fails to achieve it). The long and intricate dialogues between Job and his friends (Job 3—31) are summarily cut short by a dramatic divine intervention. Out of the whirlwind, YHWH suddenly speaks. 'Who is this that darkens counsel by words without knowledge? Gird up your loins like a man. I will question you, and you shall declare to me' (38.2–3). After so much speculation on the part of the book's human protagonists, we expect the Lord to set the record straight by revealing how he himself sees the suffering of humans. Instead, we are treated to magnificent speeches about the wonders of creation: the vastness of the cosmos, the mysteries of sea and sky, the extraordinary intricacy of the animal world (38.4—41.34). It has the desired effect of silencing Job. He acknowledges God's almighty power and the inscrutability of his purposes. He realizes that human speculation can never fathom divine mystery, and it is not only futile but impious to try. In the end, the 'problem' of pain remains unanswered and unanswerable.

But this is to begin at the wrong end. If instead we think of the book as being not about *suffering* so much as *the sufferer*, this powerful text begins to fall into place. The issue for Job is: how is he to *respond* to the string of tragedies that befall him? The loss of his lands, possessions and children is terrible enough. On top of this, his own pain threatens to break him completely. Will this tormented sufferer do what his wife suggests: 'curse God, and die' (2.9)? So the issue of the book is not theodicy but *piety*. Piety, as we saw earlier, means honouring those to whom we owe our allegiance and worship. This is the basis of Job's heroic spirituality: 'Though he slay me, yet will I trust in him' (Job 13.15, AV: the Hebrew may not mean precisely this, but it is true to Job's faith in his Maker). It cuts down for ever the poison tree of rewards, the fatal doctrine that suffering is punishment for sin, acknowledged or unacknowledged. The dialogues do not make suffering comprehensible, nor do they iron out the fundamental unfairness of so much of life. What they do is to work away at disclosing Job's integrity, and in the chaotic seas of suffering expose the rock-like solidity of his faith. When the prologue speaks of Job, the piety it describes is not a dispassionate sublimation of real experience but the gift of perseverance through it. Even among the ashes, he will not renounce faith but persists in believing in the God who will one day vindicate him: 'I know that my Redeemer lives' (19.25).

Perseverance is hard won, as anyone who has endured suffering or stood alongside others enduring it knows. As we overhear Job protesting his innocence, we feel ourselves in the presence of a man utterly abandoned, yet who is resolved to see his tragedy through to whatever end is appointed. This is of a piece with the cry of Jesus from the cross, where he takes on his lips the lament of the desolate sufferer of the Psalms: 'My God, my God, why have you forsaken me?' (Mark 15.34). It's the resolve, or at least the hope, to be faithful against all the odds, not turning our back on God even if he turns his back on us, but waiting for the time to be right when he emerges from his hiding place and addresses us.

If the book of Job is about piety rather than metaphysics, it offers important clues about the Church's ministry to and in a suffering world. Indeed, how the Church helps and supports those travelling through dark times is perhaps the best indication of how it understands its Christian vocation. This suggests that the piety of those undergoing suffering is not the only question posed by Job. It also puts to us the issue about what kind of piety is appropriate to us who are not (for the moment) enduring pain ourselves, but are called upon to be the friends and comforters of those who are.

I should like to suggest an insight drawn from the way in which some today are responding to extreme suffering. The Nazi death-camps such as Auschwitz–Birkenau have been places of pilgrimage for many people since the end of the Second World War. But what is the pilgrim to say or do in places where such unspeakable horror has been enacted? Words fail, rightly. These are not places in which to talk. Only reverent silence can begin to honour the memories of those who perished. Yet it is not enough simply to watch from afar, so to speak. We sense instinctively that there is 'work' to be done here: the mental and spiritual work that can lead to personal and collective transformation. This begins with the willingness to reflect on our own relationship to suffering and explore how transformation could happen, whether on a global, community or personal level. The phrase increasingly being used for this is 'bearing witness'.

When we 'bear witness' to someone else's pain, we do much more than simply observe it: we interiorize it, make it our own, feel what we can with another person in his or her suffering. Something like this is meant by the word 'empathy'. It is perhaps the most precious of pastoral gifts. Empathy is an attitude we can adopt whether the suffering is taking place before our eyes or far away, whether it is happening in this moment of time or has already taken place in the past. 'Witness' means noticing and being present to it in a way that makes a difference to us by engaging our compassion. As we bear witness to suffering, we hold its victims in our minds and hearts; and if we are religious people, we hold them in our prayers as well (for what else is intercessory prayer than the loving act of holding people before God?).

This implies a commitment on our part that is more than personal and subjective. 'Bearing witness' carries the sense of taking a public stance by testifying to what we have seen and heard. There is a story to be told, and it matters to the suffering, to the dead and to God that it should be heard. Christianity involves 'bearing witness' to the love of God in a way that is life-changing both for others and for ourselves (for our own belief in the gospel story we tell is strengthened by the very act of publicly telling it). Similarly, our witness to suffering begins to change at least our own attitudes towards it by becoming a matter of public story and testimony. This may happen by activating practical care and compassion for those who suffer, whether through natural causes or the inhumanity of others. It may happen as we commit ourselves to working seriously for a more just world in which war, conflict and human cruelty no longer have a place. These aims are of course central to Christian ministry.

For Christians, it is suggestive to merge these two senses of 'bearing witness'. We can do this in proclamation and pastoral care because of an incarnate God's generosity and humility in knowing this world from within. As an act of *kenosis* of which only the God of Israel is capable, the cross is the eternal sign that, as Bonhoeffer put it, 'only the suffering God can help'. We bear that sign through baptism, speak of it before the world, rest God's entire case on it. Because the Church is called to stand with the afflicted and those in pain, this is the distinctive calling of the ordained. Like the wise of Israel, we do not stand apart from suffering humanity, but squarely face the world as it is, and insofar as we ourselves know about suffering we stand with and minister to our fellow men and women, bearing witness not from a safe distance but as 'wounded healers'. The wisdom literature leads straight to the Passion narrative, and ministry is always a Passion narrative.

I was ordained priest in June 1976. It was a glorious summer. The service took place in my college chapel, a place I loved. The preacher spoke out of St John's Gospel about how love and service in the Church derive from God the Holy Trinity who is a society of love and self-giving. Afterwards, we ate and drank in the college garden in a setting that could not have been more idyllic. Three days later, a name hit the headlines dramatically and tragically: Soweto, the name that became the symbol of the struggle for racial justice in South Africa. It was a harsh reminder, at a time when I was filled with beautiful thoughts, of how the world actually was, where people were crying out of their oppression, or hunger, or disease, in the old slogan of the slave liberationists, 'Am I not a man and a brother?'

There was to me a deep synchronicity between Soweto and my being ordained priest. On the very same day that I was celebrating the Eucharist for the first time, and in awe of the holy things I was handling, people, mostly young, were being put to death: broken body and shed blood not only in the bread and wine of Eucharist, but in Soweto's streets and squares. I knew I must never forget this, how priesthood means both celebrating with and suffering with. Priesthood connects us with the whole of life. Yet I glimpsed early on that there is a particular vocation in ordained ministry to be there for victims, for the suffering, for those in pain. Archbishop Michael Ramsey said to his ordinands on retreat:

In your service of others you will feel, you will care, you will be hurt, you will have your heart broken. And it is doubtful if any of us can do anything at all until we have been very much hurt, and until our hearts have been very much broken. And this is because God's gift to us is the glory of Christ *crucified* – being sensitive to the pain and sorrow that exists in so much of the world.

Writing in the *Sunday Telegraph* just after the Boxing Day tsunami of 2004, Rowan Williams recalled the Aberfan disaster of 1966, when my generation were teenagers. I can remember, in a John F. Kennedy moment, exactly where I was when that news broke about the slurry heap that slid down the hillside on to a primary school and buried scores of young children. Rowan Williams wrote:

> I remember watching a television discussion about God and suffering that weekend – with disbelief and astonishment at the vacuous words pouring out . . . The only words that made any sense came from the then Archbishop of Wales. What he said was roughly this: 'I can only dare to speak about this because I once lost a child. I have nothing to say that will make sense of this horror today. All I know is that the words in my Bible about God's promise to be alongside us have never lost their meaning for me. And now we have to work in God's name for the future.'

At Aberfan, God himself was victim. Before we bear witness to pain, as public ministry calls us to do, God bears witness to it first. The cross and the Eucharist are the eternal signs of it. Being a minister always involves immersing ourselves in the glory and the pain of life. For when we have celebrated the praise of God, we must often sit among the ashes where Job is, and must always go outside the gate to the place of the skull, where Jesus is. There is no other way of being a priest than this.

10

Witness to the search for meaning: Ecclesiastes

———>-●-◄———

Chekhov wrote his last play *The Cherry Orchard* just before he died in 1904. His society was on the cusp of a new century, torn between the excitements of modern urban life and the fear of what would be lost by letting go of the familiar rhythms of the countryside. Chekhov knew that the old world was in its autumn. He was not to know that within a few years the entire fabric of Russia would be piteously ripped apart by revolution; yet the play foreshadows it. A family is forced to sell off its country estate to pay its debts, including a beautiful cherry orchard that is ripe not only with fruit but with development potential. The play exposes how a likeable but superficial group of people responds. They know they can't save the orchard, yet they won't face facts. In the final act, the sale is done and it is time to leave. It is October. Outside in the orchard, the axe is laid to the root of the trees – literally. The play ends with a poignant stage direction: 'A distant sound is heard, coming as if out of the sky, like the sound of a string snapping, slowly and sadly dying away. Silence ensues, broken only by the sound of an axe striking a tree in the orchard far away.'

In the book of the Bible known as Ecclesiastes or Qoheleth, the fall of the tree under sodden gun-metal autumn skies is one of the signs of a world that is ageing. In a famous passage, the world-weary 'preacher' (as the author is traditionally called) urges the young to enjoy life while they can. 'Remember your creator in the days of your youth, before the days of trouble come, and the years draw near when you will say, "I have no pleasure in them."' For him, autumn provides images not of beauty but of dissolution, decay and death. The 'days of trouble' are when 'the sun and the light and the moon and the stars are darkened and the clouds return with the rain'. The season prefigures a world running down, falling towards its end: 'Mourners will go about the streets; before the silver cord is snapped, and the golden bowl is broken, and the pitcher is broken at the fountain, and the wheel broken at the cistern, and the dust returns to the earth as it was, and the breath returns to God who gave it' (Ecclesiastes 12.1ff.). Or as Prospero says in the familiar but still incomparable speech at the conclusion of *The Tempest*:

> Our revels now are ended. These our actors,
> As I foretold you, were all spirits and
> Are melted into air, into thin air:
> And, like the baseless fabric of this vision,
> The cloud-capp'd towers, the gorgeous palaces,
> The solemn temples, the great globe itself,
> Yea, all which it inherit, shall dissolve
> And, like this insubstantial pageant faded,
> Leave not a rack behind. We are such stuff
> As dreams are made on, and our little life
> Is rounded with a sleep.

This elegiac picture of impermanence and our helplessness in the face of it is the theme of Ecclesiastes. It seems to say: there is no grand narrative in history, no overarching 'plot' being played. There is no inherent meaning in the random way in which events happen: if they are beneficent here and malevolent there, this is simply how things are. There are no exceptions, no special cases. The world does not 'feel' for mortals or owe them anything. We are born, we live, work, love, have sex, procreate and die, all in the face of an indifferent universe. There is a time for everything (3.1ff.), but if everything has its time, then nothing has time with special meaning attached to it. Everything is *chronos*, nothing is *kairos*. The cosmos simply repeats in endless cycles. There is 'nothing new under the sun' (1.9).

The Hebrew word the book uses to sum up this dispiriting state of affairs is *hebel*, literally a breath or light puff of wind. This *Leitmotif* occurs throughout the text. It draws attention to what is insubstantial and transitory (life generally), or puzzling and inscrutable (the ultimate nature of reality), or simply empty and without point (the achievements human beings pride themselves on). The epithet is piled up at the beginning and end of the book, traditionally translated as 'vanity of vanities! . . . all is vanity' (1.2; 12.8). The root meaning of 'vanity' is 'emptiness', so perhaps this is fair enough. But in modern English it feels too strong. It doesn't quite capture the tone of futility the Hebrew suggests. The book is not a prophetic diatribe against living by false values. Rather, it points to the uncomfortable truth that life in the end is absurd. It is so much air. Like Chekhov's cherry orchard, everything we invest in and that symbolizes our achievement, our security, our pride, the future, that small piece of the world we ourselves have controlled and shaped, is subject to the same law of entropy as the rest of the universe.

Qoheleth with its world-weariness and radical doubt strikes a chord in our own time. It's another example of how the wisdom literature echoes the concerns we have as contemporary men and women. Like the book of Job in the previous chapter, Qoheleth poses deep questions of theodicy: why is the world the way it is, and why do we experience it as a place without feeling or pity? In Job, the issue is sharply posed as suffering and the arbitrary way it is meted out to humans. In Ecclesiastes it is more elusive than that. For this author, good as well as evil are essentially arbitrary. What happens simply happens, whether in the wider world or within the narrower confines of a human life. Significance does not reside in events themselves; it lies in how we respond to them in the brief interval of life given to us. If there is such a thing as ultimate purpose, it is largely unknowable. The consequence is inevitable, what we could call resignation or, to borrow the language of existential thought, *Angst* or *ennui*. In this loss of meaning, all that remains is to live in the present, and do the best we can in the circumstances without asking for even the occasional glimpse of some larger purpose behind it all. G. K. Chesterton put it strikingly:

> The real trouble with this world of ours is not that it is an unreasonable world, nor even that it is a reasonable one. The commonest kind of trouble is that it is nearly reasonable, but not quite. Life is not an illogicality, yet it is a trap for logicians. It looks just a little more mathematical and regular than it is; its exactitude is obvious, but its inexactitude is hidden; its wildness lies in wait.
> (Cited in Peter L. Bernstein, *Against the Gods: The Remarkable Story of Risk*, New York: John Wiley & Sons, 1996, p. 331)

This is the world in which today's minister is largely working. We have already seen how awareness of and sensitivity to the pain of the world forms a large part of the minister's formation. There is an equally important pastoral task related to the loss of meaning that characterizes so much of our modern life. This is not the place in which to embark on an analysis of how we have got to this point in our self-understanding: the cultural and historical forces that have been at work in western Europe since at least the eighteenth century are now well known and understood. My concern here is more practical: to try to make sense of the minister's task in the difficult and exacting environment of a world that is not reasonable but not not-reasonable either. In the chapter on Daniel, I suggested that exile provided an image of the setting in which the minister is interpreting the word of God to the Church and the world. But theology is lived and performed as well as read and spoken. So here I want to focus more on the minister as a *pastor*, and ask how Qoheleth might suggest approaches to what has always been seen as core to every minister's day-to-day activity.

The book is presented as the reflection of an ageing king who has become a wiser man at the end of his long and not always happy life (1.1). But the tone of the book is instructional rather than royal. Its author styles himself *Qoheleth*, literally, someone who gathers people together, who leads the *Qahal* or assembly. Whether as teacher or preacher, the writer imagines himself as having a public ministry of some kind. Only this teacher, far from simply repeating easy formulae, engages aloud in the most searching act of self-scrutiny to be found anywhere in the Old Testament. He not only understands the dilemmas of his time: he *feels* them, submits himself to precisely the same bleak experience of *ennui* as his contemporaries. No doubt, as a man of his own time he is not exempt from the influences everyone else is subject to. More than this, he seems to be unwilling to proffer solutions to his listeners' dilemmas that are simpler than the complexity they know from their experience. If Qoheleth was a preacher, then his sermons must have been among the most honest ever delivered in the history of religion.

There are important insights here. One is that we need to be people of our own time. The incarnation offers the model of the divine entering fully into the life of humanity, not *generally* but *specifically*, at a particular time in a particular place with its specific history and culture. Ministry that is truly 'incarnational' (which is always a metaphor, never a literal description) involves the costly business of knowing, understanding and embracing what belongs to our contemporaries. The credibility of ministry depends on a deep understanding of who our contemporaries are. We need to be aware of the values by which people in our society live, not making the mistake of thinking that in an increasingly disparate nation, everyone lives in the same way. In particular – and this is the central theme of Qoheleth – we need to discern what makes for purpose, fulfilment and happiness in our age, and why. Only then can the gospel be presented with integrity as the 'answer' to human need and the fulfilment of human desire.

This task is more than learning from the cultural analysis of our society and observing trends (though both of these are important). To inhabit our own times means becoming aware of the influences at work on us too. Like our contemporaries, most of us are profoundly influenced by many, perhaps most, aspects of modernity. This includes our reliance on electronic media, expectation of instant communication and access to information. More subtle are the effects of consumerism, new sexual freedoms, the mistrust of institutions of every kind (including the Church), the collapse of traditional patterns of family life, and the overriding importance attached to personal opinion and lifestyle choice. We can't switch these off, however disturbing some of their consequences are for others and for ourselves. What matters is to establish what it means for us to live before God in this kind of world. This is not as simple as saying yes or no to it. It's more about cultivating the perspectives that enable us to celebrate the gifts and opportunities of modernity, while also establishing the critical distance we need to see it for what it is. This comes down to self-awareness as men and women of the twenty-first century.

It's an axiom of ancient wisdom that we need to know ourselves before we can embark on any other kind of knowledge. The beginning of pastoral ministry lies with the pastor himself or herself.

In particular, we are aware, as perhaps no previous generation has been, of the complexities of life, and the multitude of causes that act on us. The pastor, it seems to me, must not be afraid of complexity. If we take nothing else from what many commentators frankly admit is one of the Old Testament's most baffling books, we need at least to recognize an author who will not compromise the nature of reality by reducing it to a few easy principles which may well be comprehensible but which are certain to be wrong. We only have to open any modern scientific text, whether on cosmology, quantum physics, psychology, medicine or climatology, to realize that Qoheleth is right: the universe is indeed a complex place: beautiful, but perplexing. We share in this complexity, both as physical organisms not all of whose functions we yet understand, and as mental, emotional and spiritual beings whose mystery we cannot begin to grasp. We are 'fearfully and wonderfully made' as the psalm puts it (Psalm 139.14). As a pastor, I can't honour the complexity of another person until I acknowledge my own.

What does it mean to practise Christian ministry in this environment of complexity? More specifically, in the pastoral work of ministry, what is the outcome we are looking for?

At one level, the question hardly needs an answer. Ministry is literally 'service'. To serve and care for others is an end in itself. Their help, nurture, support and love need no other justification than our common humanity. To be a fellow human being is to recognize and honour the image of God in that person, however broken, debased or obscured the divine image may seem to be. It is not a question of whether we are ordained or lay, Christian or non-Christian, a member of a caring profession or simply a good neighbour, relative or friend. We care because we are fellow members of the human family. Altruism is, or ought to be, a universal human law.

However, to practise Christian ministry *publicly* in the name of the Church gives particular significance to pastoral care, as it gives it to every other activity that church leaders engage in. That significance is *religious*. It carries Christological meaning because it is done as an expression of the love of God in Jesus Christ. Whether we intend it or not, it is an aspect of the Church's mission, and this is how it is perceived. This gives the act a different quality. It gives it a directly religious content. Jesus says of the works of mercy: 'Just as you did it to one of the least of these who are members of my family, you did it to me' (Matthew 25.40). To feed the hungry, clothe the naked, care for the sick and visit the imprisoned is to minister to Christ *incognito*. It therefore carries a redemptive dimension.

We need to pursue how meanings are attached to the activity of ministry. At one stage of my ministry, I considered embarking on a course to help me develop my pastoral skills. There are now many excellent training programmes for pastors and spiritual directors, but in those days, in that part of England, the only option was to do a course of counselling. I was fortunate to get the advice of someone who made me examine my assumptions carefully. He said to me:

> You are a priest. That is your public role. People come to you for help and support not in spite of your priesthood but because of it. Even those with no religious affiliation will seek you out knowing who and what you are, and expecting you to be true to it, whether explicitly or implicitly. You will benefit from counselling skills, but you can never work to value-free humanistic assumptions. Your ordination gives everything you do a religious meaning. You may wish you were a counsellor and

less marginal to society than a parish priest may seem to be. Yet your public office confers unique opportunities which your position on the margins may actually help. Live out what you are, a person whose core meaning is Christ-shaped.

Looking back, I realize that this conversation was defining for me as a young priest. It helped me to see that if a minister always carries religious meaning for people, then his or her mission must always be to help them find religious meaning for themselves. However it is expressed, it comes down to this: the discovery of Christian purpose in life. I don't think this implies that the goal of ministry is to offer some grand narrative that will chart the mystery of things. That would be to fall into the trap I mentioned above of imposing a template over reality and collapsing down its complexity. Indeed, the very elusiveness of the cosmos probably *is* its grand narrative. Rather, I believe it means helping people construct points of meaning around those places where their lives touch the world and the world touches them. This is a more modest project, but it is attainable because it is led not by metaphysical speculation but by the evidence of experience understood in the light of faith in God. In a world that seems absurd, this is Qoheleth's strategy.

Does this inductive approach to Christian ministry rob it of real content? Not at all, if we keep our nerve. We best do that by not underestimating how large things are built up out of small things. In his own ministry, Jesus seems to be something of a miniaturist. When his followers want a grand gesture such as accepting the accolade of kingship or coming down from the cross, he resolutely refuses it. What is striking in the Gospels is the quality of modesty and hiddenness that pervades his words and works. His compassion for the poor and outcast, his words for the common people, his healing of the maimed and damaged, his call to a group of nobodies to be his followers, his washing their feet in an upper room – it is through simple acts like these that the kingdom of God is glimpsed. In the same way, I believe that faithful ministry is mainly a matter of offering tiny Christ-shaped glimpses in word and action. It may seem futile to imagine that this can ever make a lasting difference. Yet over time, these glimpses build up into a coherent picture of a world in which Christ himself is present. This is how faith is so often born in human lives: without spectacle or drama, the result of painstaking, patient ministry over many years. We can never know what the fruits of our prayers and our efforts will be.

French literary theorists use the word *bricolage* to describe a building or work of art that is constructed out of whatever materials are to hand. The term has been borrowed by literary theorists to refer to the way the bits and pieces of decon-structed narratives, the detritus of worn-out stories, are put together. Qoheleth's world, like ours, is precisely like this, or it feels that way: deconstructed, meaningless, without any clear shape or form except what he is capable of imparting to it. But although the preacher hovers on the brink of despair, he never capitulates to it. Emptiness, absurdity, 'vanity of vanities' does not have the last word in the book. At the very end of Ecclesi-astes he draws back from the abyss. The cloud of unknowing is pierced by a shaft of light. It's impossible to know whether this conclusion is the work of the preacher himself attaining some resolution, or the hand of a later editor for whom the medita-tions of Qoheleth were too radical to be left as they stood. It does not matter. The canonical text marks the conclusion of at least this stage of a lifelong journey of exploration. 'The end of the matter; all has been heard. Fear God, and keep his com-mandments; for that is the whole duty of everyone. For God will bring every deed into judgement, including every secret thing, whether good or evil' (Ecclesiastes 12.13–14).

In this, the writer does not go beyond what he knows. Even in a world whose forces appear to act randomly upon us, it is possible to construct oases of structure and sense through the way we live life. To fear God and to keep his commandments is to refuse to 'lead lives of quiet desperation' as Henry David Thoreau described the human condition. Rather, it's to believe that purpose, direction and meaning are attainable through faith in God. Ordained ministry is the vocation to live out before the world the belief that there is coherence and purpose in things. Just as ministry is public witness to suffering, it is also public witness to the search for meaning. Doing this authentically is always a hard and exacting task; and perhaps never more so than in our time and culture. We feel our own fragility; like Paul, we know that 'we have this treasure in clay jars' (2 Corinthians 4.7). Yet also like him, the impossibility ever of wholly fulfilling this calling draws us into the source of the strength we need. Our very brokenness and perplexity only makes it clear that 'this extraordinary power belongs to God and does not come from us'. The ordeals Paul goes on to describe are in his case the result of human agency. For us today, the same symptoms can be a consequence of living in a pain-ridden, baffling world. 'We are afflicted in every way, but not crushed; perplexed, but not driven to despair; persecuted, but not forsaken; struck down, but not destroyed' (2 Corinthians 4.8–9).

Why is it worth persevering with? Paul gives us his answer: 'so that the life of Jesus may also be made visible in our bodies'. In that most succinct of statements lies the aim of Christian ministry. It's ultimately the work of the risen Jesus himself, alive in the world. This is to take us beyond the point reached by Qoheleth, even in his conclusion. Because of the resurrection, St Paul can make his own magnificent response to a world he may at times have felt was not so different from

Qoheleth's 'vanity of vanities'. His answer to the preacher is all we need to hear as we persevere against all the odds in our God-given task: 'We do not lose heart' (2 Corinthians 4.16).

11

Witness to joy: the Song of Songs

Summer ordinations in the Church of England often coincide with Wimbledon fortnight. I once preached about tennis at an ordination – no small achievement for someone with my athletic prowess. I said that it was the most theological of sports because not only do you *serve* in tennis, but every game, set and match starts out from *love*. My attitude to sport was coloured when, on my second day at prep school, a hot September afternoon, I was frogmarched with 29 other boys out on to a rugby pitch. We sat down on the parched ground to be taught the rules of the game by – well, perhaps I'd better not say whom. He began his exposition by saying: 'Boys, always remember that the object of a game is to enjoy yourself.' Within a week, the misery of cold, wet, muddy afternoons confirmed that this was not altogether true. But he was right about the theory. We need enjoyment, recreation, laughter; we are *homo ludens*, people who play. It's how we learn and grow. It's how we tap into our creativity and enlarge the imagination (which is why we speak of *recreation*, a word I used in the brief excursus on the Rule of St Benedict when we looked at the *terroir* of the minister in Chapter 7). Far from being a way of escape, to play well is to enter into reality. It is to experience a kind of freedom.

In the book of Proverbs, there is a magnificent passage I have already referred to, in which playing isn't simply seen as a human activity, but belongs to the nature of God himself.

Lady Wisdom, whom we have already met earlier in this book, is pictured as being with God at the beginning, as if she is the mind and imagination of God, fashioning the heavens and the earth, giving birth to life (Proverbs 8.22–31). In the famous painting of creation in the Sistine Chapel where the spark of life passes from God's finger to Adam's, Michelangelo has placed a beautiful woman by God's side: not Eve, probably, nor the Virgin Mary, but the figure of Wisdom, poised to help God in his mighty work. I think the text is telling us that creation is not *work* at all, but *play* on God's part. 'I was . . . his darling and delight, playing continually in his presence, playing on the earth . . . while my delight was in mankind' (8.30–31, NEB). It's an image of laughter in heaven and creation as an act of playfulness and joy. God did not have to make the world. It was his choice: *we* are his choice. And if we could open our eyes to this sunrise of wonder at our own existence, we too, like God, would dance and play.

The gospel is an invitation to be re-created and to find in Jesus our delight. In the cross and resurrection of Jesus there is a new creation. Paradise lost has been restored to us and made more glorious. Jesus says that receiving the kingdom of heaven is to embrace this new world God is making. It's to dance when he pipes to us; it's to leap for joy because we are being healed; it's to sing when anyone turns back to God; it's to feast at his table like royals; it's to assist at a wedding; it's to become like little children. These are all images of pleasure and play. You could say that the Church is called to be a community of delight, who are discovering what it means, as the *Westminster Shorter Catechism* puts it, 'to glorify God and enjoy him for ever'. Like Thomas in St John's Gospel, a reading often used at ordinations, we acclaim the risen Jesus as our Lord and our God, and pass from the shadows into the full light of day (John 20.19–29).

The ordained ministry of the Church is a visible focus of all this, as it is of everything else that the Church proclaims. And if we ask what is at the *heart* of priestly ministry, I reply that it is *to preside over the Church's praise of God*. The Church is never more a community of delight than when we gather to offer our praises in the Eucharist. This is the significance of *eucharistia*, thanksgiving, as the redemptive principle of life. And we offer praise not only on our own behalf but, we believe, for the whole human family; indeed, for the whole of creation. In the Eucharist, we celebrate the love shown us in Christ and we anticipate the promised new creation. We come to the table of God as to a banquet. Whether we are rich or poor, quick-witted or dull, weak or powerful, old or young, Christ invites us to his table as honoured guests, makes us kings and queens as we feast on the bread and wine of heaven. The liturgy is godly play. It opens our eyes and makes us wise. It imagines that the kingdom of God is already among us and invites us to live as if it were and because it is. In giving shape and voice to the play of God's people, priests have a uniquely privileged role.

Clergy are there for many things. We have seen how much of ministry concerns the dark and desperate places of life where people are overwhelmed by tragedy, suffering and pain, and are struggling with failure, facing death, longing for purpose and meaning. Into these places the priest comes as *alter Christus*, as Christ himself, bearing his grace and truth. Again, because the Church stands for public faith, the priest is a sign of God's judgement and mercy in the world, where the gospel word needs to be spoken into the issues of our time: conflict, poverty, politics, social ethics, saving our planet. For every minister, ordination is a sacred and inescapable vocation to be immersed in the world as Jesus was, and to keep faith and hope alive. We have commented many times in this book on the fact that it can be hard to be a priest in a society such as ours, so ambivalent about religion. The explorer and writer Laurens Van der Post writes about meeting a despairing White Father in the Congo who said, 'There is another great age of darkness closing in on the life of man, and all that we can do is to create little fortresses wherein the authentic light of the spirit can be kept burning. Then, one day, when men wish to reach out for light they will have places in which to find it.' Perhaps we have already reached that day.

However pessimistic the outlook for organized religion, however unsure the clergy are becoming about their role, the answer is not to be merely dutiful, or to think that seriousness is the same thing as solemnity. The joyless religion many of our forebears endured at the hands of the clergy showed how easily the gospel of joy could become fatally distorted. William Blake saw this for what it was in his *Songs of Experience*:

> I went to the Garden of Love,
> And saw what I never had seen;
> A Chapel was built in the midst,
> Where I used to play on the green.
>
> And the gates of this Chapel were shut,
> And 'Thou shalt not' writ over the door;
> So I turned to the Garden of Love
> That so many sweet flowers bore.
>
> And I saw it was filled with graves,
> And tombstones where flowers should be;
> And priests in black gowns were walking their rounds,
> And binding with briars my joys and desires.

Blake points us (as he does in all his poetry) to a more ecstatic vision of life in which everything is underpinned by celebration and delight. In this, he is one of the poets in the English language who is truly 'eucharistic'. What is the lesson for the ordained, with the vocation to hold up to a world devoid of hope visible signs of faith and meaning? That they do this most convincingly when they recall the Church to her joy in God as creator and saviour. The best – perhaps the only – antidote to despair is thankfulness.

If there is one book of the Hebrew Bible that has delight as its principal theme, it is the Song of Songs. Like Proverbs and Ecclesiastes, it is ascribed to Solomon, and since he was the legendary patron of wisdom, the Song seems to ask to be read as wisdom literature. We have seen how close observation of the natural world and its beauty is characteristic of Hebrew wisdom; indeed, when the narrator wants to describe Solomon's wisdom, he mentions both his composition of 1,005 songs, and his love of nature (1 Kings 4.32–33). The book is a collection of sensuous love songs that charts the tides of erotic love from desire to consummation. Perhaps they originated in the lyrics that we know from parallel Egyptian texts that were sung at wedding banquets.

Because of its sensuous content, and its lack of explicit reference to God, the Song of Songs proved troublesome when it came to determining whether it should be included in the third division of the Hebrew canon of authoritative books, the Writings. In what sense could this be sacred scripture? Its place in the canon was probably secured by the argument that the book was not *really* about love between human beings at all, but about the relationship of Israel with her God. Until the rise of critical biblical study in the early nineteenth century, Jewish and Christian interpretation has consistently veered towards the allegorical and mystical. Medieval writers such as the famous twelfth-century Cistercian preacher St Bernard excelled in elaborating each detail of the text in terms of an aspect of the spiritual life of the Church or the individual soul.

It is tempting to see in this tendency the discomfort that religious people usually feel when faced with explicit human sexuality – and the Song of Songs is explicit. However, allegory does not solve the problem, for if it is permitted to use the imagery of sexual desire to speak about union with God, then that desire is at once divinely affirmed and validated. If desire for sexual union with another person is God-given, then it is perfectly apt, as many writers on erotic love now point out, to see in it not simply an *image* of spiritual desire, but an actual *expression* of it, conscious or unconscious, and however chaotic it can become. The celebration of sexual intimacy in the Song of Songs is one of the ways the canon affirms the goodness of things. When the New Testament writer bids his male readers to 'love your wives, just as Christ loved the church' (Ephesians 5.25), the implications for how both human sexuality and divine love are to be understood are illuminating and rather startling.

However, I want to ask not so much what the book has to say about sexual relationships, but to reflect on it as a book of delight and ask how this might inspire the Church's ministry today.

One way of reading the Song in the context of its near neighbours in the Hebrew Bible is to see it as 'opposite' to the book of Job. That book draws us into the heart of darkness and asks us to ponder the mystery of human pain. In the same way, the Song of Solomon invites us into an Eden of delight so that we can reflect on the mystery of goodness and love. Just as Job does not explain the 'problem' of suffering but presents it as the ultimate riddle of the cosmos, neither does the Song moralize or theorize about the nature of love. Like suffering, it is a fact of our existence. But perhaps there is an important difference of nuance between suffering as a 'given' and love as a 'gift'. Suffering is seen by most people as a 'problem' (though as I have said in the chapter on Job, the book is more about the *sufferer* than suffering as an abstract idea). But while theologians point out that love is as much of a mystery as suffering, it seems oxymoronic to call it a 'problem': why explore and analyse when what we are called to do is to enjoy? Yet it is important to recognize that joy and woe are the twin mysteries of life. Love defies explanation in the same way as pain. 'Joy and woe are woven fine, a clothing for the soul divine,' as William Blake put it. These are our constant companions on the journey: always present, never understood.

We have seen that public ministry is very much concerned with 'mystery'. Whether as a theologian, evangelist, celebrant at the liturgy, spiritual guide or pastor, the minister is dealing all the time with God's wise, loving but mysterious purposes for his creation. The New Testament speaks of being called to be 'stewards of the mystery of God', and one definition of ministry is that it is making the mystery of God present and alive to people. Like the Rosary, life has its joyful mysteries, its sorrowful mysteries and its glorious mysteries, and all of these are the daily work of the clergy. And while sorrow occupies a large amount of space in both the outer and the inner worlds of every minister, a biblical theology of grace insists that these must be seen within the even larger space that belongs to joy and glory. If the Eucharist is the sign and seal of transformation, this is because the most fundamental act which a human being can ever perform is to offer thanksgiving. In Hebrew thought, things are made holy by giving thanks: this is what it means to 'bless'. The primary mode of being for the Church and for its ministers is gratitude and praise, celebration and delight. Easter invites us into Blake's garden of love. The Eucharist is a place of *play*. 'Even at the grave we sing *alleluia!*'

In the chapter on Job, I explored the idea that one of the functions of the minister is to 'bear witness' to suffering. I suggested that the Church publicly 'notices' that people are in pain and cares about them because God himself 'notices' and cares – infinitely. I think we can say that in the same way, public ministry 'notices' joy and celebrates it, because it's a sign of God's presence. Prayer for the world's needs and those in pain, the sacramental ministry of healing, liturgy with the sick and dying, vigils at times of crisis or mourning, funeral and memorial services are among the many public ways in which the Church 'bears witness' to suffering. In the liturgical cycle the rites of Holy Week are the annual reminder of how suffering is God's concern before it is ours.

But the Church publicly bears witness to joy as well. It does this through rites such as baptism, confirmation and marriage, national and local celebrations, thanksgivings at special occasions and of course the liturgical seasons of Christmas, Epiphany and Easter. Without 'tidings of joy', ministry would not confront the powers of chaos with the proclamation that God intends his world to become a place of what the Hebrew Bible calls *shalom*: that rich, God-given wholeness and fulfilment that is only very inadequately captured up by our English word 'peace'. To announce God's kingdom is the ultimate joyful mystery of which the minister is privileged to be a steward.

In my work with clergy, and in my own experience, I have seen how easily joy and gratitude are eroded by the abrasions, conflicts, pressures and disappointments that all ordained men and women experience over a lifetime of ministry. The loss of a sense of living in a privileged vocation can be very noticeable. Of course, the 'first fine careless rapture' that follows ordination doesn't last for ever. Like marriage, it is necessary to renegotiate the vocation regularly in the light of changed circumstances. Above all, this needs to happen in the light of the inward changes that take place in the human psyche over the years. I am not the same person my wife married more than 30 years ago; neither am I the same person on whom a bishop laid hands under a Norman chancel arch in a parish church in Oxford a year later. Yet the recovery of joy is essential if the ordained ministry is to emerge from the crisis of confidence it is currently experiencing in all our churches today. How might this happen?

The Church is engaging with a number of generic approaches such as pastoral reorganization (when it is not a euphemism for requiring clergy to make bricks out of straw), better support, more professional approaches to conditions of service, and regular review. All these are welcome when they are offered intelligently and not imposed as if they were the latest systemic cure-all. However, the morale of the clergy is as much a spiritual as a systemic issue, as writers on pastoral ministry from Gregory the Great onwards have known. It may seem eccentric to invoke the Song of Solomon to the clergy dilemmas of the twenty-first century. Yet the Song is of a piece with everything we have seen in the wisdom tradition that calls the wise to be attentive and present to what is happening in the world and in their own lives. In the Song, that call is to be alive to joy, which is the same as saying that it is a call to be truly *alive*.

There is a perceptive insight in the diaries of the twentieth-century French-American writer Julien Green:

Last night, (I) listened over the air to a part of *Don Giovanni* which is being given at Aix. After an hour I went to bed, no longer *hearing* a music I know too well and am so deeply fond of. I might almost say that I was familiar with the leading airs before knowing how to read, for my sisters used to play and sing them in our old rue de Passy flat. All my life, these delightful themes have been with me, following me in joy as well as in sadness; they have already lost their novelty for me, and it is a pity; I fear to hear them too often, not to find them each time lovelier,

fresher; I dare not write that I fear to tire of them . . .
What wouldn't I give to hear *La ci darem* for the first
time! That intoxicating *first time* that in all spheres gives
us something we will never find again . . . I have always
thought that our joy in heaven will be made up of this,
that we will see God for an eternal *first time*; there will be
a one and only time that will never cease, there will never
be the sad thing linked to duration: repetition. (*Diary
1928–1957*, London: Collins and Harvill, 1964, p. 214)

(Green perhaps thought he was nearing the end of a long and
productive life when he wrote those words, though he went
on to become almost a centenarian.)

It is poignant to realize that every joy that surprises us is
also a loss because we can never again know it for the first
time. Yet perhaps there is a clue in Green's way of speaking
about an 'eternal first time'. Might it not be possible to cultivate the habit of becoming so present to the moment that it
brims with something like the freshness and joy it had 'the
first time'? This may be hearing *La ci darem*, seeing Northumberland spread out before you from the summit of the
Cheviot, or (to evoke the language of the Song of Solomon),
being reunited with your lover or friend. T. S. Eliot speaks in
'Little Gidding' of knowing the place 'for the first time', as if to
enter into a familiar experience once again, bringing to it our
attention and our lived experience, is indeed to encounter it
in a new way. This is what the early eighteenth-century French
spiritual writer Jean-Pierre de Caussade called, in one of those
great phrases that seem exactly right, 'the sacrament of the
present moment'.

It is this kind of spirituality of the 'first time' that I believe
we need to recover in the ordained ministry. The Song of
Solomon imagines the setting where 'journeys end in lovers'
meeting' to be a garden. Surely not just any garden, but *the*

garden, primordial Eden, the place of every beautiful and joyous first time. The Song is saying that joy has the ability to transport us back to those innocent beginnings where life and happiness were first given, the paradise where, ever since, our human hungers and longings are directed. In the prophets and again in the Revelation to John, history is recapitulated by bringing creation back to a garden once more, where the tree of life bears fruit and leaves for the healing of the nations (Revelation 22.2). To be 'surprised by joy' is to be transported into a garden of delight, not simply to remember but to experience as if for the 'first time' the present moment of God-given happiness and contentment.

I wrote earlier about the perils faced by religious professionals, among them, over-familiarity with sacred things. The antidote, I think, is to reawaken the sense of 'first time' about the work of ministry. Perhaps this is especially true in its later years. It means becoming attentive again to what we are doing before God when we preside at the Eucharist, read the Bible, preach, care for people, comfort the needy, baptize, marry, bury, and do the thousand other things that ordination means. It means reconnecting, in all this, with the sense of privilege that came with ordination. Witness to suffering is critical here, and there are clergy who can speak, paradoxically, about how their ministry was renewed by some deep and painful encounter with suffering. They say that this comes from the shock of reality that tragedy brings, how it often calls its witnesses to review their entire lives.

But witness to joy is, if anything, even more important. It too is about reality. Like tragedy, joy strips away fantasy and illusion. It calls us back to what is truly worth being alive for, what ultimately matters in this life. So joy has a redemptive quality, both because blessing is redemptive in itself, and because it tells the truth and points not to itself as some kind of end, but to its ultimate source. In the climactic line of the book in which a wisdom lesson is drawn from the lovers' ecstasy in each other, the text tells us where delight stands in the great scheme of things. 'Love is strong as death . . . Many waters cannot quench love, neither can floods drown it. If one offered for love all the wealth of one's house, it would be utterly scorned' (Song 8.6–7). Like so much of human experience, the divine is not explicitly present in the lovers' delight. They are each other's fulfilment. Yet God is immanent in all of it, the ever-present spring of all that is lovely and good. And this includes all that is lovely and good in the personal experience of ministers themselves.

Witness to joy is witness to love, and therefore it is witness to God. This is the story the ordained ministry exists to tell. We have seen how the work of the minister is to be an interpreter of what God is doing, often silently and unseen, in the lives of human beings. It is frequently a case of saying, with Gerard Manley Hopkins: 'I greet him the days I meet him, and bless when I understand.' These words come from his poem 'The Wreck of the Deutschland', written in the aftermath of a tragedy. But they are equally apt in the face of joy. Recognizing and articulating it, trying to 'know the place for the first time', is one of the best habits to covet because it leads to Hopkins' redemptive movement from meeting, greeting and understanding to blessing.

All of ministry is summed up in that, and all of wisdom.

Epilogue: mining for wisdom
An ordination sermon on Job 28

In the days when coal was king, there was an entire language that used to be spoken by the pitmen of the Durham and Northumberland coalfield. 'Pitmatic', as it is called, has wonderfully arcane words like 'clarty', 'galloway', 'kennah', 'tarry-tout' and 'yakka', useful for Scrabble. Another is 'cuddy'. On and off the north-east coalfield, 'cuddy' is an affectionate nickname for Cuthbert, our native saint. On Lindisfarne you can collect little pieces of fossilized wood called cuddy beads on the beach opposite St Cuthbert's island; you can watch the cuddy ducks on Inner Farne. But in the pitmatic spoken near Alnwick where I was once a parish priest, a cuddy was a pitman's ass, and, by extension, a fool; if they called you one, it was not a compliment. In east Durham, however, to be cuddy wifted means being left-handed or ambidextrous, and that has the nuance of being rather clever.

The Durham Miners' Gala service is our annual reminder that this cathedral and the mining industry are inseparable. One of the most moving places in this building is the memorial where the names of hundreds of men who perished down the mines are recorded. A miners' banner hangs in the south transept like an icon in an Orthodox church. Our first reading from the book of Job is a familiar miners' text that features a sort of Bible pitmatic with its obscure language about swaying miners suspended precariously in pits deep below the surface of the earth. It tells of mining operations in the ancient world:

139

gold, silver, copper, iron, precious stones – everything is harvested from the fiery, dangerous depths of the earth: everything, that is, except coal – and one other commodity so elusive that you can't mine it or dredge it up from the sea. You can't buy it or barter it – you can't even put a value on it, for it is beyond price. You will hear rumours of it but you won't find it, travel to the ends of the earth but you will come back empty-handed. Only God knows its place, says Job, understands its secret.

This rarest of harvests, says Job, is wisdom. Even though it has been there from the beginning when the world was created and God saw it and searched it out, it remains hidden from mortals. We cannot find it on our own. Yet there is a way to it, open to everyone. 'The fear of the Lord, that is wisdom; and to depart from evil is understanding.' To be wise is to know your place in the world and before God. It's to recognize that God requires of us our reverent allegiance – this is what 'the fear of the Lord' means. As a consequence, it's to know what it means to live well as a person of integrity and mercy, justice and truth. And because God is the source of wisdom, because he *is* wisdom, to be wise means becoming like him. Becoming like him means knowing him, offering him our loyalty and love.

Wisdom has been the theme of our ordination retreat over these past few days. I have tried to suggest that ordained ministry is a calling to help other people become wise and live in the light of God's invitation to know and love and worship him. The Bible is a story not of rigorous duty but of rich delight, for its theme is the gracious, generous movement of God towards us and towards his world. Wisdom is a gift of God before it is a requirement of human beings. The New Testament speaks about Jesus as the Word and Wisdom of God made flesh, visible and tangible among us. He comes as God only wise to show us what it is to walk in the way of

wisdom. He comes as God only love to rescue us from our
folly and re-create us so that we can realize our destiny, which
is to bear the image and likeness of God in the world:

> O loving wisdom of our God!
> When all was sin and shame,
> a second Adam to the fight
> and to the rescue came.
> (John Henry Newman)

To help others become wise means being, or becoming, wise
ourselves. This is the calling to which these men and women
are to be ordained this morning. Public ministry in the
Church has never been more exacting than today when most
of our contemporaries think the Church is irrelevant and our
talk about God incomprehensible. More and more we are
'singing the Lord's song in a strange land'. Yet we do not lose
heart. This calling, to make people wise, and our society wise
to the threats and opportunities facing it, is an immeasurable
privilege. In the retreat we looked at the story of King
Solomon at the outset of his reign. At this defining moment
God appears to him and invites him to ask for the gift he most
needs. Solomon resists the obvious self-driven requests:
wealth, victory, a long life. Instead, he prays for wisdom to
govern his people well, for, he says, 'I am only a little child; I
do not [even] know how to go out and come in.' We may hope
that those taking part in the forthcoming G8 summit come to
Scotland in that spirit. They will certainly need the wisdom of
Solomon, and the worldwide crowds of demonstrators are
not going to forgive them if they don't at least ask for it. And
as for our deacons today, there is no other prayer to offer than
the humble request for the understanding and discernment
that only God can give.

As you embark on a lifetime of service in the ordained ministry, let it begin and end with this: the wisdom that is the fear of the Lord. Seek her out, not as something to be unearthed by human effort, but deep in the unfathomable mines of God. Nurture her, cultivate her, let her be alongside you as she was alongside God in creation. Recognize, as Solomon did, that God gives what he commands; what you lack will be yours if you ask for it. You would not be human if you did not feel that all you can do today is to hold out empty hands to God. Today, St Thomas' Day, is for all who are only too aware of fragility and doubt, fightings within and fears without. But God's way is to place jewels in a rubbish heap, and give the keys of the castle to cowards, as Teresa of Ávila put it. He has brought you to this point. He will give you the wisdom you need. In the risen Jesus he comes to us on this first day of the week in word and sacrament, he invites you to acclaim him and offer yourselves to him in those magnificent words of recognition: 'My Lord and my God!' All this is what we shall shortly be asking for you in the prayer of the Church at the heart of this ordination service.

The great South African writer Alan Paton wrote to a godson on his confirmation day in words I find very apt for an ordination. They encapsulate how the mystery of God is entrusted to human beings who are becoming wise, who know themselves, who are humble enough to ask to be forgiven, who only want to serve well and to be faithful to Christ all their lives. He writes about how discipleship is a continuous process of willing self-offering, of failing to live up to those promises, of turning back and being welcomed and restored, and then of joyful renewal as life begins again. He ends by saying:

> Take and accept them all, be not affronted nor
>   dismayed by them,

they are a net of holes to capture essence, a shell to
   house the thunder of the ocean,
a discipline of petty acts to catch creation, a rune of
   words to hold one Living Word,
a ladder built of sticks and stones whereby they hope to
   reach to heaven.

Today is another stage on that privileged, God-given journey.
Travel well, and God speed.

Durham Cathedral   *3 July 2005*
Job 28.1–6, 20–28
John 20.24–29

A note on books

―――⇒●⇐―――

On wisdom
This can only be an introductory selection of books, though I am glad to include among them one by a former Dean of Durham, my Old Testament teacher Eric Heaton. In addition, there is a wide range of commentaries on the wisdom literature, too numerous to mention here.

Crenshaw, James L., *Old Testament Wisdom: An Introduction*, Atlanta: John Knox Press, 1981.

Davidson, Robert, *Wisdom and Worship*, London: SCM Press, 1990.

Day, John, Gordon, Robert P. and Williamson, Hugh G. (eds), *Wisdom in Ancient Israel*, Cambridge: Cambridge University Press, 1995.

Ford, David and Stanton, Graham (eds), *Reading Texts, Seeking Wisdom*, Grand Rapids: Eerdmans, 2003.

Heaton, E. W., *Solomon's New Men: The Emergence of Ancient Israel as a National State*, London: Thames & Hudson, 1974.

Hoglund, K. G. et al. (eds), *The Listening Heart: Essays in Wisdom and the Psalms in Honour of Roland E. Murphy*, London: Continuum, 1987.

Melchert, Charles F., *Wise Teaching: Biblical Wisdom and Educational Ministry*, Harrisburg: Trinity Press International, 1998.

Morgan, Donn F., *The Making of Sages: Biblical Wisdom and Contemporary Culture*, Harrisburg: Trinity Press International, 2002.

Murphy, Roland E., *The Tree of Life: An Exploration of Biblical Wisdom Literature*, Grand Rapids: Eerdmans, 2002.

Von Rad, Gerhard, *Wisdom in Israel*, London: SCM Press, 1972.

Weeks, Stuart, *Early Israelite Wisdom*, Oxford: Clarendon Press, 1994.

On ministry

If there is one book on ministry I wish I could have written myself, it would be Michael Ramsey's classic *The Christian Priest Today*. Any minister could profitably read it through once a year. Among the others, it is good to be able to mention a number by past and present colleagues from whom I continue to learn.

Brown, Rosalind, *Being a Deacon Today: A Theological and Practical Explanation*, Norwich: Canterbury Press, 2005.

Brueggemann, Walter, *Cadences of Home: Preaching Among Exiles*, Louisville: Westminster John Knox Press, 1997.

Carr, Wesley, *The Priestlike Task*, London: SPCK, 1985.

——, *The Pastor as Theologian: The Integration of Pastoral Ministry, Theology and Discipleship*, London: SPCK, 1989.

Clitherow, Andrew, *Renewing Faith in Ordained Ministry*, London: SPCK, 2004.

Cocksworth, Christopher and Brown, Rosalind, *Being a Priest Today: Exploring Priestly Identity*, Norwich: SCM-Canterbury Press, 2002.

Countryman, William, *The Language of Ordination: Ministry in an Ecumenical Context*, Philadelphia: Trinity Press International, 1992.

A note on books

Croft, Steven, *Ministry in Three Dimensions: Ordination and Leadership in the Local Church*, London: Darton, Longman & Todd, 1999.

Jamieson, Penny, *Living at the Edge: Sacrament and Solidarity in Leadership*, London: Mowbray, 1997.

McGregor, Bede and Norris, Thomas (eds), *The Formation Journey of the Priest: Exploring 'Pastores Dabo Vobis'*, Blackrock: The Columba Press, 1994.

Mason, Kenneth, *Priesthood and Society*, Norwich: Canterbury Press, 1992.

Pritchard, John, *The Life and Work of a Priest*, London: SPCK, 2007.

Ramsey, Michael, *The Christian Priest Today*, London: SPCK, 1972.

Wright, Frank, *The Pastoral Nature of the Ministry*, London: SCM Press, 1980.